THE QUAY TO THE COVE

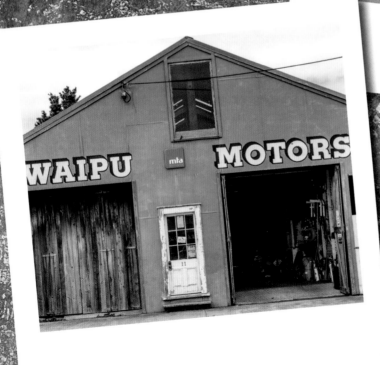

THE QUAY TO THE COVE

COASTAL CUISINE

LINDY DAVIS

NEW HOLLAND

café
restaurant
& bar

THE COVE

Open 7 days
a week!!

Summer Is
Coming !!

OPEN 7 DAYS
7am till late!

CONTENTS

9 FOREWORD

13 INTRODUCTION

14 BEGINNING

19 BREAKFAST BY THE SEA

35 PADDOCK TO PLATE

97 COASTAL CATCH

135 DRESSINGS AND SIDES

145 SWEET THINGS

179 COCKTAILS

188 INDEX

191 ACKNOWLEDGEMENTS

This book is dedicated to everyone who has a personal goal and the resolve to make it happen. Most of what we ultimately accomplish is the product of creative energy, alongside hard work.

FOREWORD

Lloyd and I spent time together travelling Europe and experiencing the wonders and delights that many different countries have to offer. The most memorable fare being Morocco's tasty tagines, Spain's paella and sangria, Thailand's tantalising curries, Italy's perfect, home-made pasta, traditional Ozzie barbecues, the best of British fare including pies and Cornish pastries and all that France has to offer from its amazing sauces, beef bourguignon and steak tartare that Lloyd loved with a passion.

We sampled rich and diverse foods from all over the world and managed to incorporate the best into our restaurant menu at the Duke of York.

Lloyd's high-octane energy, enthusiasm and passion for food are second to none. He takes great delight in entertaining guests with an infectious smile, and an eye for detail that's been relentless over his 26 years in hospitality.

I'm looking forward to trying all the recipes in this formidable and fabulous book and to bring a taste of New Zealand to the UK.

Craig Revel Horwood
Runner-up *Celebrity Chef* UK; Judge *Strictly Come* Dancing UK; Judge *Dancing with the Stars* NZ; Theatre Director UK, ITV cooking series host

INTRODUCTION

'You have to try my steak tartare, it's amazing.' Lloyd Rooney flashed me a winning smile from the kitchen and so began our friendship over several long lunches, toasting the unique and special charm of a coastal paradise in New Zealand.

This book is essentially the result of Lloyd's inspiration. It's a story about food. *The Quay to The Cove* is divided into different parts.

Beginning is a nostalgic glimpse at the past and the gastronomic delights of London and Europe. It tells the story of how Lloyd came to New Zealand and started The Cove café. Breakfast by the Sea is a collection of small plates from The Cove and The Quay kitchens.

Paddock to Plate is all about supplying the produce from their farm at Highgate Hill, about local food sources and the commitment to supplying the restaurants with local produce whenever possible.

Coastal Catch is a look at New Zealand's abundant local seafood transformed into wonderful ocean delicacies at The Cove in Waipu.

Sweet Things, the delights that we enjoy at the end of a meal. Discover the delicious desserts that are served at both restaurants. Sweet Things also documents how Lloyd founded his second restaurant, The Quay, at Whangarei.

This cookbook, *The Quay to The Cove*, brings together Lloyd's recipes as well as those of chefs from his restaurants. The recipes are the successful merger of exotic European cuisine with unique flavours from the South Pacific.

Explore, eat and be inspired!

BEGINNING

Not all those who wander are lost.
J.R.R. Tolkien

Nothing could be closer to the truth after meeting restaurateur, Lloyd Rooney. Growing up in Brighton in the UK, Lloyd was home-schooled from the age of twelve until the end of his senior year.

Cooking and baking became part of his daily routine and he quickly developed a natural interest in food. Dark chocolate cake was just the beginning, followed by savoury scones and then his first attempt at beef stew.

Just old enough to do the grocery shopping, he learnt budgeting skills and realised the only way to beat the odds was to further educate himself.

Lloyd studied for a degree in Social Science at London University and lived at Goldsmith halls of residence. He financed himself through the three-year degree with an evening job as a 'red coat' VIP usher at the Theatre Royal in Drury Lane.

He personally escorted the Queen to her box for the Royal Variety performance and was front of house usher for the Queen mother's 90th birthday celebration at the Palladium.

Although enjoying the pomp and splendour associated with the theatre, a nagging concern that he hadn't accomplished enough in the academic arena saw Lloyd embark on an intense one-year law conversion course.

Despite a diagnosis of dyslexia at the age of 24, his tenacity paid off and he received a job offer with a law firm in Aldgate.

'I felt like an actor switching between roles. By day I was a lawyer advising my clients and by night I was working long hours in the hospitality industry.'

His world irrevocably changed in 1992 when he met Australian Craig Revel-Horwood, who was in the core cast of the musical, Cats. It was due to Craig's encouragement that Lloyd's real passion with food began.

'We would go to the markets and hunt out all the fabulous cheeses and smoked meats imported from Europe.'

When he finally made the decision to tell his parents he was gay, Lloyd was given an ultimatum that gave him little choice. He left home and suffered a five-year silence from his parents.

As Lloyd's life with Craig became more entrenched in theatre and restaurant dining, he developed a greater interest in food, and worked part-time at renowned French bistro, Café Delancey in Camden Town, London.

'I remember the menu so well, particularly a couple of my favourite dishes like the mille-feuille

champignon, a mushroom-filled pastry entrée and the lamb signature dish carré d'agneau.'

The chef made his own gravlax and Lloyd learnt the art of curing salmon with just the perfect ratio of salt, sugar and dill.

His next job took him to The Engineer in London's Primrose Hill, owned by Laurence Olivier's daughter, Tamsin. The menu focussed largely on seasonal farm-to-table dishes. He particularly enjoyed the haddock kedgeree, and smoked salmon fish cakes with cumin and fresh coriander. As head of house, Lloyd gleaned a wealth of hospitality experience, and consequently a much greater appreciation of fine European wines.

Craig's job had transitioned from choreographer to resident director of the musical Miss Saigon that played at the West End Theatre and the Lido. The role required extensive travel and Lloyd loved the opportunity to visit France.

He was instantly captivated by the food and lifestyle that Paris offered and spent Sunday afternoons browsing the Paris flea market, listening to the haunting voice of Edith Piaf playing in his favourite café, Chez de Louisette. It was a far cry from the drudgery of law and working long hours in hospitality.

Having always had an eye for stylish art and homewares and after a particularly joyous afternoon drinking Rosé on the banks of the Seine, Lloyd hatched an idea that would take him in an entirely different direction.

'I returned to London feeling completely disconnected with my job. I didn't really know what I wanted – I was clearly drawn to food but I couldn't see where it would take me. On a whim, I visited a psychic and before I had a chance to sit down, he told me "you're not meant to be in an office job, if that's why you're here". I thought a great deal about what he'd said as I cycled home.'

After a few weeks of reflection, Lloyd resigned from his law job and hung up the apron at The Engineer. Spontaneously, he signed a lease on a shop in Chelsea and in 1998 the interior design business, Revelloyd, was born.

In search of stylish pieces for his new Chelsea shop, Lloyd combed the markets obtaining objects-de-art and sourcing unique pieces through private collections or at auction.

'Creativity comes from tapping into something deep inside yourself and when it comes to interior design, I believe you just have an eye for it.'

Lloyd travelled across Europe sourcing specialty items for clients. He regularly attended the Maison and Objet Art and Homewares exhibition in Paris, and Lille Braderie, Europe's largest annual street market.

He found intricate painted lamps and hand-woven rugs from Isfahan, glassware from Italy, art from Morocco and leather furniture from Scandinavia.

'I would arrive with an empty van and, by the end of the weekend, it would be overflowing with treasures I'd found at the markets. But by far the biggest treat was gorging on mussels and chips at my favourite café in Paris.'

His reputation as a designer grew, and before long his clientele came from all over Europe and the United States.

'I adored the travel especially around Essaouira and Marrakech and found myself falling in love with food all over again. I learnt how to make Moroccan lamb and almond tagine and a delicious home-made pate from Provence.'

The interior design business was running on auto-pilot and Lloyd needed a new challenge. He was naturally drawn to exotic cuisine and the following year teamed up with friend and business partner Brendan Connolly to open his first Moroccan/French fusion restaurant, The Duke of York, in St Johns Wood.

'Brendan owned a French café in Covent Garden and our chef was French, so it seemed natural to gravitate towards French cuisine.'

Their signature dish was wood pigeon and almond pastilla, a traditional Moroccan pastry dish filled with almonds and wood pigeon. Chicken and preserved lemon tagine was also a mainstay on the restaurant menu.

For the next three years Lloyd successfully juggled the interior design business alongside the restaurant.

Eventually Lloyd sold his share of the restaurant to Brendan and opened a second design studio in Islington. Lloyd expanded the interiors business and the referrals continued. There were regular trips to Iran, Sweden, Africa and various parts of Europe in search of artistic homewares.

'I liked to blend antiquities with contemporary European design. I've always believed you can showcase several things together from various cultures.'

His second shop attracted an even bigger client base and Lloyd was kept busy assisting celebrity clientele including actors Kevin Spacey and musician Dido, who engaged him to furnish their homes.

Craig spent more time ensconced in theatre and television, joining the judging panel for British television show *Strictly Come Dancing*, as well as the New Zealand series *Dancing with the Stars*. He was also runner-up in the popular UK series, *Celebrity MasterChef*.

With so much time spent in his interior design business, Lloyd missed the hospitality business and looked for a way to combine his genuine love of food and his interior design skills.

'I visited new cafés and spent time sampling wonderful French and Dutch cheeses and home-made pates. The love of good country-style food never really left me.'

Despite twelve years together, Lloyd and Craig found themselves increasingly busy with their own independent lifestyles and inevitably moved in different directions.

'My relationship with Craig came to an end but we've always remained good friends and whenever I'm in London we make an effort to catch up.'

Craig moved to directing several major shows and is a renowned British television personality with his own cooking series.

And as fate would have it, Lloyd met a down-to-earth Kiwi who successfully enticed him to move in an entirely new and distant direction.

BREAKFAST BY THE SEA

*What nicer thing can you do for somebody
than make them breakfast?*
Anthony Bourdain

Breakfast often means different things to different people. *The Quay to The Cove* menu offers a combination of breakfast and brunch options catering for even the fussiest palate.

From breakfast smoothies to nutritious light dishes, there is plenty of diversity using seasonal ingredients as often as possible.

SMOOTHIES

Easy to make and fast to digest, kick start the day with a healthy smoothie. It's the best way to consume fresh nutrients when time is at a premium. As with any recipe, it's a matter of taste and you can change the ingredients depending on seasonal availability. Handfuls of fresh fruit or detoxifying greens will keep you feeling awake and energetic.

An Omni Blend V blender is used at The Cove, but a Nutri-bullet or equivalent works just fine.

Serves: Each smoothie makes a single glass
Preparation time: 5 minutes

VITA BERRY BLAST

2 handfuls of frozen or fresh
   blueberries
1 handful of frozen raspberries
½ banana
1 handful of spinach
6 ice cubes
250 ml (8 fl oz) coconut water

METHOD

- Place the ingredients into a mixer and blend for 90 seconds or until the required consistency is achieved.

Note: Remember rapid blending can cause overheating, so add additional ice if necessary.

DETOXICATOR

½ apple, skin on, pips removed
½ pear, skin on, pips removed
½ banana
1 slice pineapple
handful of spinach
6 ice cubes
200 ml (7 fl oz) coconut water

METHOD

- Cut up the fruit into bite sized pieces. Add to a blender with
- the rest of the ingredients and blend for 90 seconds or more, taking care not to overheat the appliance. If the smoothie is a little thick, add extra ice or a little water.

PEACHY BREAKFAST

1 peach, pip removed
½ fresh mango (or handful
   frozen mango pieces)
½ banana
small scoop of hazelnuts (or
   almonds)
3 teaspoons flax seeds
250 ml (8 fl oz) coconut water
2 tablespoons natural
   unsweetened yogurt
   (optional)

METHOD

- Cut up the fruit into bite sized pieces.
- Add to a blender with the rest of the ingredients and blend for 90 seconds or more, taking care not to overheat the appliance. If the smoothie is a little thick, add extra ice or a little water.

SMOOTHIES

ACTIV8OR

½ banana
handful of grapes
½ pear, pips removed
handful of walnuts
6 ice cubes
200 ml (7 fl oz) coconut water
scoop protein powder
  (optional)

METHOD

- Cut up the fruit into bite sized pieces.
- Add to a blender with the rest of the ingredients and blend for 90 seconds or more, taking care not to overheat the appliance. If the smoothie is a little thick, add extra ice or a little water.

PINEAPPLE CRUSH

2 slices pineapple
2 nectarines, stone removed
handful of grapes
½ banana
sprinkle of goji berries
6 ice cubes
200 ml (7 fl oz) coconut water

METHOD

- Cut up the fruit into bite sized pieces.
- Add to a blender with the rest of the ingredients and blend for 90 seconds or more, taking care not to overheat the appliance. If the smoothie is a little thick, add extra ice or a little water.

VANILLA PEAR HEAVEN

1 pear, pips removed
handful of spinach
1 teaspoon coconut butter
1 teaspoon vanilla essence
200 ml (7 fl oz) almond milk
6 ice cubes
1 tablespoon oats

METHOD

- Cut up the fruit into bite sized pieces.
- Add to a blender with the rest of the ingredients and blend for 90 seconds or more, taking care not to overheat the appliance. If the smoothie is a little thick, add extra ice or a little water.

EGGS BENEDICT

A classic favourite and the ingredients can be adapted to suit. Salmon or grilled haloumi are healthy alternatives to bacon for the non-meat eaters.

Serves 4
Preparation time: 30 minutes

HOLLANDAISE SAUCE
4 egg yolks
1 tablespoon of lemon juice
250 g (9 oz) melted salted butter
pinch of salt

1½ L (2½ pt) of hot water
1 tablespoon white vinegar
4 large eggs
8 rashers streaky bacon
large bunch baby spinach, washed and drained
500 ml (16 fl oz) boiling water
sea salt and freshly ground black pepper
4 ciabatta rolls

METHOD
- To make the hollandaise sauce, mix the egg yolks and lemon juice in a food processor or blender. Slowly add the hot melted butter at a slow consistent stream and season to your liking. Season with salt and set aside in a warm place until you require it.
- In a 2 L (3½ pt) pot, add hot water and white vinegar. Bring to the boil and then lower temperature to a gentle simmer.
- Crack eggs one at a time just above the water surface (break egg into a cup, if you are worried about puncturing the yolk, pour into the pot from the cup).
- Cook the eggs for 2 minutes until the whites are opaque but the yolk is still wobbly. Using a slotted spoon, remove eggs and place on an absorbent paper towel.
- To wilt the spinach, place in a sieve and pour the boiling water over the top. Drain completely. Season with salt and pepper.
- Serve eggs on toasted ciabatta with crispy bacon, spinach and top with hollandaise sauce.

CARLI'S RAWNOLA

An energy-packed breakfast granola, delicious served with poached fruit in the winter and fresh berries in the summer. This recipe was created by one of our locals.

Serves 2–4
Preparation time: 30 minutes

GRANOLA
280 g (10 oz) soft pitted dates
120 g (4 oz) rolled oats (or mulberries as a gluten free/paleo alternative)
50 g (2 oz) shredded coconut
25 g (1 oz) cranberries
15 g (½ oz) chia seeds
15 g (½ oz) hemp seeds
38 g (1½ oz) chopped brazil nuts
1 tablespoon cinnamon
1 tablespoon coconut sugar
1 tablespoon coconut oil

POACHED NECTARINES
4 nectarines
2 tablespoons coconut sugar
1 teaspoon pure vanilla extract
1 star anise pod
1 lemon rind, chopped
500 ml (16 fl oz) water

TO SERVE
2–4 spoonfuls unsweetened yoghurt
edible flowers (optional)

METHOD
- To make the granola, place all ingredients into a mixer and pulse into small clumps. Store 'rawnola' in a glass jar in the refrigerator to keep fresh.
- To make the poached nectarines, place nectarines in a pot with coconut sugar, vanilla, star anise and chopped lemon rind.
- Cover with the water and bring to the boil, slowly reducing heat to a simmer for 10 minutes. Nectarines should be soft but still intact when pierced with a knife.
- Set aside to cool. Any remaining syrup can be added as an option to sweeten the rawnola or alternatively discarded.
- Peel nectarines and slice into quarters.
- Serve nectaries on top of rawnola with a spoonful of unsweetened yoghurt and decorate with edible flowers if you wish.

WHITEBAIT OMELETTE

Whitebait is a New Zealand delicacy best sourced fresh.

Serves 4
Preparation time: 20 minutes

INGREDIENTS

4 whole eggs
15 ml (½ fl oz) cream
50 g (2 oz) New Zealand whitebait
1 teaspoon Kaitaia Fire Chilli Sauce
1 tablespoon fresh chives, chopped
1 tablespoon parsley, chopped
sea salt and freshly ground black
    pepper
1 teaspoon clarified butter
1 tablespoon olive oil
micro salad greens, for garnish
fennel sprig, for garnish

METHOD

- Whisk the eggs with the cream. Add the whitebait, chilli sauce, chives and parsley. Combine until evenly mixed. Salt and pepper to taste.
- Heat a heavy-based non-stick frypan until hot, then add the butter and olive oil to the pan.
- Pour the egg mix into the hot pan, carefully moving the mix away from the sides. When the omelette is two-thirds cooked, place under a grill or put into a hot oven for one minute.
- Remove and transfer to a plate and serve with a few microgreens and a sprig of fennel on the side.

Note: The omelette should be served creamy and still soft to touch. If whitebait isn't in season, replace with mushroom duxelle (p. 87) and finish with Danish feta crumbled on top.

STEWED FRUIT WITH TOASTED BRIOCHE

There is plenty of fruit in this recipe so, if you prefer, you can opt to use less sugar.

Serves 4–6
Preparation time: 1 hour

INGREDIENTS
8–12 fresh strawberries
8–12 fresh blueberries
8–12 fresh raspberries
350 g (12½ oz) caster sugar
400 ml (13 fl oz) water
2 cinnamon quills
3 star anise
6 cardamom pods
1 orange, peel and juice
500 g (17½ oz) peeled rhubarb, cut
   into 2 cm (¾ in) pieces
150 g (5 oz) dried apricots
150 g (5 oz) dried figs

TO SERVE
4–6 tablespoons mascapone
4–6 tablespoons Lemon Curd (p. 159)
4–6 loaf brioches, toasted and cut with
   a cookie cutter
sprikle icing sugar, to garnish

METHOD
- Wash and place all the berries into a large flat dish.
- To prepare the poaching liquor, combine caster sugar, water, cinnamon quills, star anise, cardamom pods and the orange peel and juice in a pot. Mix together and bring the liquid to a simmer.
- Add the rhubarb, dried apricots and figs and poach on a low heat until just tender.
- Remove the fruit from the syrup and place on top of the berries.
- Pour the syrup over the poached fruit/berries and leave to cool.
- Toast the brioche under a grill or in a toaster.
- Swirl the lemon curd on each plate. Place the fruit with syrup on the lemon curd and the brioche on top. Sprinkle with icing sugar. Serve with a dollop of mascarpone on the side.

Note: Make sure you leave the cardamom pods and quills in the syrup as this adds more flavour. Replace with any seasonal fruit you like. Frozen berries will also work. The stewed fruit from this recipe is also delicious with the Rawnola.

FALAFEL AND HUMMUS PLATTER

This is a traditional middle-eastern recipe with a beetroot twist. Falafel can be served on baked flat bread or in a pita.

Serves 2
Preparation time: 40 minutes

FALAFEL
500 g (17½ oz) chickpeas, cooked
1½ tablespoons chopped garlic
1½ tablespoons dried cumin powder
½ teaspoon cayenne pepper
1½ tablespoons baking powder
125 g (4 oz) chickpea flour
125 ml (4 fl oz) lemon juice
50 g (2 oz) flat leaf parsley, chopped
1 medium-sized beetroot, peeled and grated
sea salt and freshly ground black pepper
vegetable oil, for frying

HUMMUS
1½ cups chickpeas, soaked overnight
125 g (4 oz) tahini paste
2 tablespoons olive oil
1 tablespoon cumin
1 tablespoon garlic, crushed
4 tablespoons lemon juice, freshly squeezed
sea salt and freshly ground black pepper

TO SERVE
flat bread
Dukkah (p. 76)
micro salad greens
Romesco Salsa (p. 76)
avocado oil
Greek unsweetened yoghurt or labneh (optional)

METHOD
- To make falafel, blend the chickpeas in a food processor so that they are still slightly chunky.
- Place the chickpeas, garlic, cumin, cayenne pepper, baking powder, chickpea flour, lemon juice, parsley and raw beetroot in a mixing bowl.
- Combine the ingredients, making sure the spices are evenly distributed. Season to taste.
- Portion the falafel mix into small 50 g (2 oz) balls and deep fry at 175°C (347°F). You can also shallow fry in a very hot pan if you don't have a deep fryer.
- To prepare the hummus, cook the chickpeas in salted water until completely tender. Once cooked, drain and add to a food processor together with the tahini paste, olive oil, cumin, crushed garlic and freshly squeezed lemon juice. Blend to get the desired smooth consistency.
- To serve, spread the flat bread with hummus, add the falafel, an assortment of dukkah and a sprinkle of salad greens. Serve the romesco salsa and avocado oil in separate bowls. If using yoghurt, serve in a bowl for people to add as they wish.

Note: This recipe makes enough for a generous platter. Any falafel mix left over can be stored in the refrigerator for up to 4 days.

MEDITERRANEAN TOAST

This is best using fresh seasonal vegetables. If you can't source the ingredients below, then substitute using blanched beans, red onion and zucchini.

Serves 1–2
Preparation time: 15 minutes

INGREDIENTS
1–2 fresh corn cobs, husks removed
2 vine-ripened tomatoes, sliced
2 avocados, sliced
small handful micro greens
small handful of watercress
2 tablespoons Citrus Vinaigrette
   (p. 136)
2 slices toast, thick sliced, 5-grain if
   possible
2 tablespoons Basil Pesto (p. 143)

OPTIONAL EXTRAS
2 poached eggs (p. 107)
1 tablespoon pomegranate seeds
2 slices smoked salmon

METHOD
· Bring some water to the boil in a saucepan. Add the corn cobs and cook until the kernels appear yellow and plump, about 6–8 minutes. Remove and cut the cobs into bite size chunks.
· Combine tomatoes, avocados and corn pieces with micro greens and watercress and add the vinaigrette. Mix well.
· Toast the bread, and spread a tablespoon of basil pesto on top of each slice. Arrange the salad mix on top. Dob some basil pesto around the platter or plate for decoration.
· As optional extras, add a poached egg, pomegranate seeds or slices of smoked salmon.

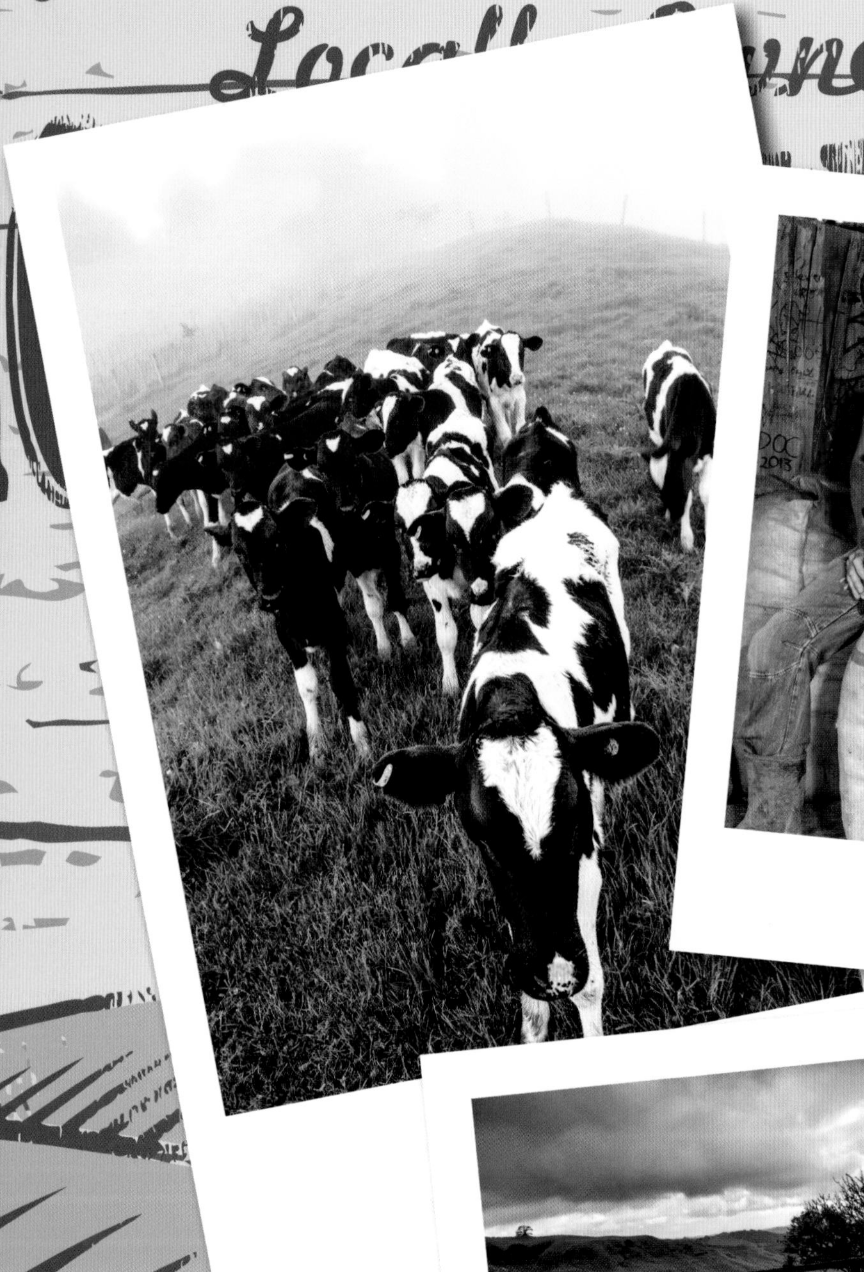

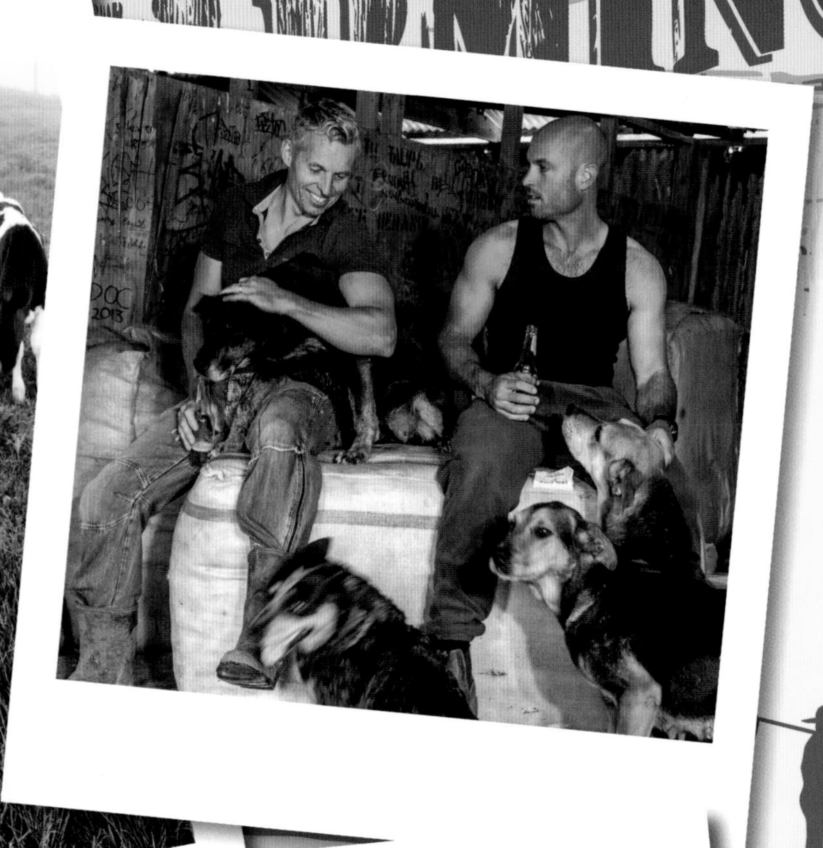

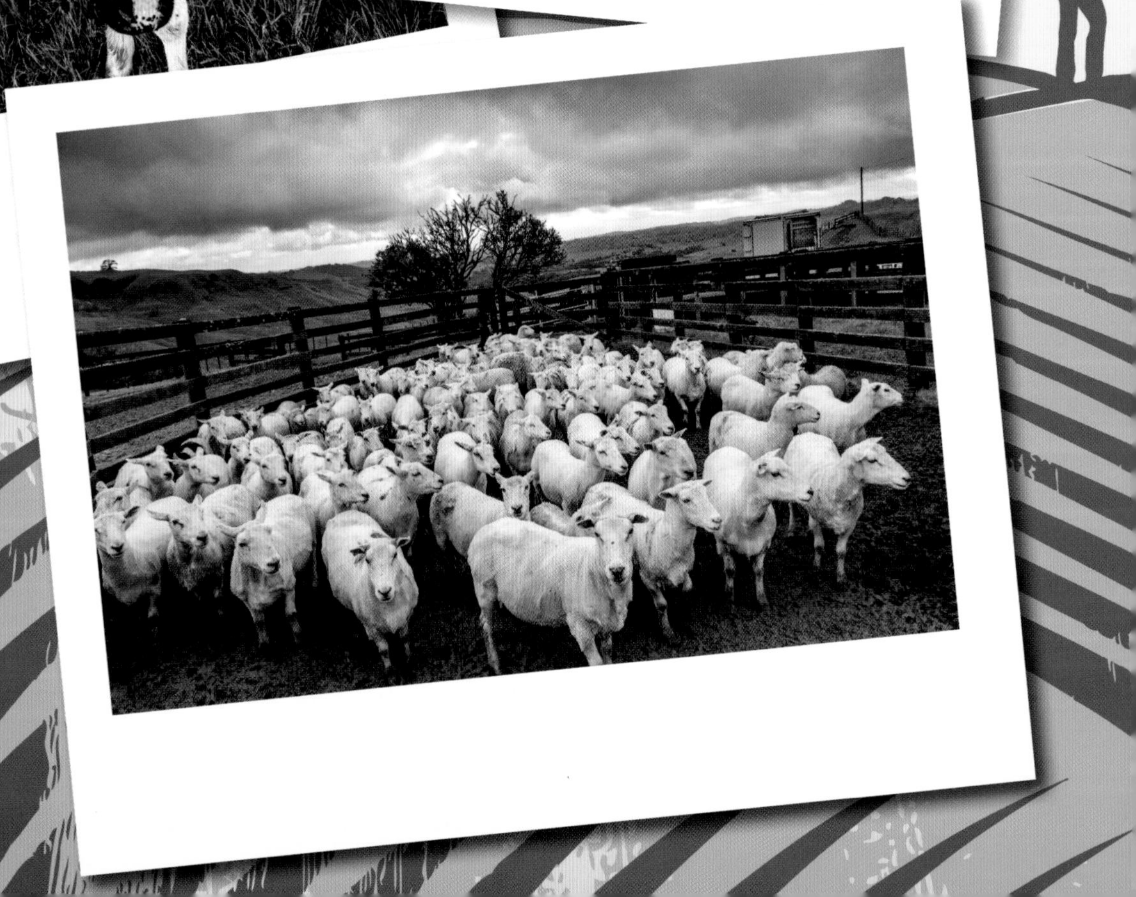

PADDOCK TO PLATE

*A friend once described me as a potato. Put me on the ground anywhere
and I'll sprout.*
Lloyd Rooney

Travelling through Europe, Michael Fraser just happened to be in the right place at the right time. He was staying at his sister's flat and spotted Lloyd outside his interior design store in London. After an impromptu drink, the chance meeting was meant to be.

'When Michael turned up in my life basically things spun upside down,' said Lloyd of the meeting.

Lloyd took time off work to show Michael the highlights of London, closely followed by a holiday in Greece and Turkey before Michael returned home to New Zealand.

Lloyd was at a crossroads, and following gut instinct made the bold decision to leave London in search of a fresh start in the Antipodes.

Arriving in the land of the long white cloud was one thing, but he soon found himself thrown in the deep end, gumboots and all.

Michael's passion lay in farming, specifically cattle, while Lloyd's farming experience amounted to zero.

Together they researched potential farms in New Zealand and found a piece of land they loved, Highgate Hill in Wairamarama, south of Auckland.

Surrounded by green rolling countryside, the 2200-acre sheep and beef farm was one of the largest holdings close to Auckland.

'When you see an opportunity you've got to have the guts to take it and be flexible enough to see where it goes. So that's what we did.'

Lloyd admits it was an eye opener coming from London to wind up in the heart of rural New Zealand. The local community was very tight knit, just twelve families within a 30-kilometre radius. The closest towns, Pukekohe and Tuakau, bore no resemblance to any Lloyd was accustomed to in the UK.

'I was in a state of shock by the time we reached the farm, and it didn't help that the locals had already dubbed it "Brokeback",' explains Lloyd.

The farmhouse interior was stark. Lloyd set about making some changes; adding wallpaper, luxurious rugs and pendant lights, transforming the space into something stylish.

'Although the "gay farmer" label initially identified us, it in no way defined us and we soon proved we could easily hold our own.'

Michael was the farm manager and together with co-worker Kevin Webb, helped cover-up some of Lloyd's early farming mishaps.

Lloyd was fast tracked into Farming 101, with six dogs and a tractor. He was determined to learn all facets of rural life, including moving cattle, drenching, crutching and repairing fences.

'I'm certainly not the best shearer and the ones I cut aren't pretty. Most of them look like they've had a really bad hair day.'

Michael discreetly suggested Lloyd might be better suited in the kitchen, cooking hearty meals for the shearing gang. He happily switched roles, producing eggs benedict and trays of beef lasagne with Sicilian sauce for the shearers breakfast.

Lloyd learnt to operate the tractor, and obtained his C2 truck licence. Given the quantity of meat they consumed on the farm, he thought it would be useful to learn to do home kill.

'I honestly think if we all killed our own animals for food, there would be a lot more vegetarians.'

Lloyd made an effort to keep in touch with a number of families in the district and was elected President of the Wairamarama farming community.

He initiated an annual party in the local hall to get everyone involved and proposed a 'Heaven and Hell' theme for the inaugural event, appearing in stubby shorts and knee-high Wellington boots, large white feather angel wings and his body brushed top-to-toe in gold glitter.

'I've arrived!' he beamed.

Determined to embrace his new role on the farm, he entered into the spirit of things and adopted a pet goat named Krusty and a calf with a tuft of frizzy hair they named Mugatu.

'There's so much comedy and honesty at the farm and it's definitely not for the faint hearted. There's no correlation between the hours worked and the income earned, but I like to put my heart into everything I do, so I gave it my best.'

Michael likes the solitude and space that comes with being on the land, and finds working alongside animals very rewarding. Lloyd is naturally more of a social creature thriving in a busy environment and interacting with people.

'You have to love the great outdoors because there's an element of loneliness working on a farm. I juggle a few jobs en-route to the gym, like buying calves, visiting the vet, and picking up pigs or piglets. I'm usually covered in mess and often smelling a bit feral,' said Lloyd.

After nine years on the farm, Lloyd was keen to find a way back into the world of hospitality and through a fortuitous meeting with friends at the gym, he learned about a restaurant opportunity in Northland. They'd been looking to bring the Highgate Hill beef and lamb to the wider market and thought with Lloyd's background experience in the UK, a café would be ideal.

They drove north to Waipu and despite the bleak weather, Lloyd and Michael loved the spot.

They were shown the site where the original Cove Beach House, an iconic two-storey white weatherboard holiday accommodation once stood. The next time they visited The Cove, it was bathed in sunshine and that took it to a whole new level.

On hearing that Waipu was originally settled by Scottish Highlanders who made the intrepid trip from Nova Scotia to Northland in 1851, Lloyd commented: 'I figure if they can spend two years crossing treacherous seas to create a thriving community in Northland, then we can make the three-hour drive a couple of times a week.'

The Cove café became a reality and opened with an innovative menu using fresh local seafood and beef and lamb sourced from Highgate Hill farm.

CAULIFLOWER, SAFFRON AND PARMESAN SOUP

Cauliflower is grossly under-rated and sometimes for good reason, but combined with the right ingredients, it has the ability to provide delicious subtle flavours to any dish.

Serves 4–6
Preparation time: 45 minutes

INGREDIENTS
100 g (3½ oz) butter
1 tablespoon olive oil
1 onion, sliced finely
1 cauliflower, sliced finely
2 teaspoons saffron threads, soaked in
   cold water
500 ml (16 fl oz) cream
50 g (2 oz) Parmesan, shaved
salt and pepper, to season
8–10 corn chip crackers (optional)

METHOD
- Soak saffron in a shallow bowl of water for 30 minutes. Heat the butter and olive oil in a saucepan until the butter has melted. Add the onion and cauliflower and cook on a low heat until tender.
- Drain water and add the soaked saffron, cream and reduce heat a little further.
- Continue to stir the soup, adding shaved Parmesan and season with salt and pepper.
- Serve in bowls with corn chip crackers if you wish.

Note: The key to this soup is not to overcook the cauliflower to keep it tasting fresh and vibrant.

STEAK TARTARE

Lloyd fell in love with steak tartare during a visit to Paris. On one occasion a French Michelin-star trained chef came to stay at their Highgate Hill farm property and taught him how to prepare it.

Serves 2–4
Preparation time: 25 minutes

INGREDIENTS

600 g (21 oz) fresh steak (eye fillet or rump)
4 egg yolks
4 tablespoons light olive oil
1 tablespoon Dijon mustard
3 tablespoons tomato sauce
¼ quarter onion, very finely chopped
1 tablespoon capers
4–5 anchovy fillets, finely chopped
sprig fresh parsley, finely chopped
4–6 dashes Tabasco sauce
6–8 dashes Worcestershire sauce
sea salt and pepper
fresh crusty bread, to serve
Anchovy Mayonnaise (p. 140), optional, to serve

METHOD

- To mince the meat, trim off any fat and put it through a mincer on a fine setting for eye fillet or a more coarse setting for rump steak. If you don't have a mincer, finely chop the meat by hand, being careful not to over process it.
- Add the egg yolks and oil to the mince and mix thoroughly.
- Add mustard, tomato sauce, onion, capers, anchovies and parsley and blend evenly.
- Add Tabasco and Worcestershire sauce. Salt and pepper to taste.
- Divide into four portions and serve with toasted crusty bread and anchovy mayonnaise as an appetizer or divide into two portions and serve as a main.

Note: If chopping by hand, put the meat in the freezer for thirty minutes to chill and make it easier to finely chop. Mince or chop the steak when you're ready to serve as it can discolour if left for too long.

CALF'S LIVER WITH BACON AND MUSHROOM

This dish was served at Joe Allen's in Covent Garden and was the perfect meal to have after a show. The delicate combination of seared liver and mushroom with a hint of truffle oil is delicious. Allow about 100 g (3½ oz) of liver per person.

Serves 4–6
Preparation time: 50 minutes

INGREDIENTS

streaky bacon rashers, 1–2 per person
250 ml (8 fl oz) cream
1 tablespoon beef jus (or powder)
2 tablespoons wholegrain mustard
8–12 Portobello mushroom caps
4 teaspoons butter, ½ teaspoon per
  mushroom cap
8–12 garlic cloves, 1 per mushroom
  cap
6–8 sprigs of thyme, leaves chopped
1 calf (or lamb) liver, 100 g (3½ oz per
  person), thinly sliced
2–4 tablespoons olive oil or butter
2 tablespoons plain (all-purpose) flour
sea salt and freshly ground black
  pepper
drizzle truffle oil (optional)
ciabatta, cut into wedges and toasted

METHOD

- Heat a pan and cook the streaky bacon until crisp. Set aside.
- Heat the cream in a saucepan and reduce by half. Add the beef jus and combine.
- Stir in the wholegrain mustard, being careful that the sauce doesn't boil.
- Preheat the oven to 180°C (350°F).
- Heat a frypan and lightly sauté the butter and garlic. Remove from heat.
- Place the mushrooms on an oven tray and baste them with the butter and garlic.
- Sprinkle with generous amounts of thyme leaves on top of the mushrooms and roast until cooked through.
- Dust the liver slices in flour seasoned with salt and pepper.
- Add oil/butter in a saucepan. Turn to high and fry the liver quickly turning after a minute, making sure to cook both sides of the liver. As a guide it should be medium rare.
- To serve, place the liver on top of the roasted mushroom and partially ladle over the mustard sauce. Top with crispy bacon, a drizzle of truffle oil (optional) and wedges of toasted ciabatta.

CHILLED GAZPACHO SOUP WITH BEETROOT AND BLUE CHEESE

Lloyd first tried this soup in Seville, Spain. It was served with chopped peppers, croutons and a hard cheese. Cove café adapted this recipe to use seasonal baby beets and Mahoe blue cheese. Gazpacho is best kept in the refrigerator to chill.

Serves 6
Preparation time: 30 minutes

THE SOUP

1 large cucumber, peeled and
   deseeded
10 overly-ripe tomatoes
¼ red onion, chopped
2 large red peppers
1 teaspoon cumin
1 teaspoon garlic
½ teaspoon Kaitaia Fire Chilli Sauce
   (or chilli sauce of choice)
¼ teaspoon Worchestershire sauce
1 lime, juice
1 tablespoon fresh basil
½ tablespoon red wine vinegar
sea salt and fresh ground black
   pepper, to taste

TOPPING

2 golden baby beets
2 red baby beets
sea salt and freshly ground black
   pepper
4–6 sprigs fresh basil (or thyme)
1 tablespoon blue cheese, crumbled

METHOD

- To make the soup, combine all the ingredients together in a blender and season to taste. Refrigerate for two hours to chill, allowing the flavours to settle.
- Preheat oven to 180°C (350°F).
- Lay beets on tin foil and sprinkle with salt, pepper and thyme. Wrap individually in the foil and place in the oven for 35–40 minutes or until soft (a skewer should go through the beets easily when cooked).
- Remove from oven and cool. Peel and dice using gloves to stop your hands from staining.
- To serve, pour the gazpacho into bowls. Add diced golden and red beets and crumbled blue cheese. Garnish with sprigs of thyme on top.

BEEF CARPACCIO WITH TRUFFLE OIL AND PARMESAN

This simple yet elegant dish is the Italian version of Steak Tartare. It is ideal as a summer entrée especially with a delicious bottle of chilled Fleurie, or a rounder red in the winter months.

Serves 6
Preparation time: 30 minutes

INGREDIENTS

300 g (10½ oz) mid loin beef eye fillet, trimmed
6 free range eggs, poached (see p. 89)
50 g (2 oz) Parmesan, crumbed or shaved
drizzle truffle oil
Anchovy Mayonnaise (p. 140)
handful of micro herbs, rocket (arugula) or basil
pinch of sea salt

METHOD

- Roll the beef firmly in cling film and place in the freezer for an hour (to make slicing easier).
- Place a sheet of baking paper on the plate that you plan to serve on.
- Unwrap the beef and slice very thinly with a very sharp knife. Place the slices separately in a circular pattern on the sheet of paper. Refrigerate until time to serve.
- Remove the beef from the refrigerator and allow to come to room temperature, about 20 minutes.
- To serve, arrange the slices of beef on each plate, add a soft poached egg in the middle and shaved Parmesan scattered around. Add a drizzle of truffle oil and anchovy mayonnaise. Finish with micro greens, rocket or basil and a pinch of sea salt.

Note: Be careful with the truffle oil as it can be very overpowering – you don't need much to get the flavour.

SEARED BEEF SALAD

We use beef from our Highgate Hill farm and recommend grilling the meat rare-to-medium. The sweet and savoury flavours in the dressing are a highlight.

Serves 6
Preparation time: 45 minutes

ASIAN DRESSING
1 tablespoon garlic, crushed
1 tablespoon ginger, peeled and crushed
1 spring onion (scallion), chopped
1 stalk lemongrass, chopped
125 ml (4 fl oz) lime juice
125 ml (4 fl oz) lemon juice
250 ml (8 fl oz) Kikkoman soy sauce
125 ml (4 oz) sweet chilli sauce
50 g (2 oz) washed coriander (cilantro)
   leaves, including roots
50 g (2 oz) Vietnamese mint leaves
125 ml (4 fl oz) sesame oil
250 ml (8 fl oz) light olive oil

SALAD
1 red capsicum (bell pepper)
1 yellow capsicum (bell pepper)
1 orange capsicum (bell pepper)
1 Lebanese (telegraph) cucumber,
   seeds removed
¼ small red cabbage
1–2 tablespoons vegetable oil
500 g (17½ oz) steak (scotch, sirloin or
   eye fillet)

GARNISH
2–4 shallots (French onions), thinly sliced
olive oil, for frying
cashew nuts

METHOD
- Blend the dressing ingredients together and add seasoning as required. Pass through a medium sieve to remove any fibre. Refrigerate overnight.
- Wash and finely slice the salad vegetables. Season and lightly coat the steak with oil.
- Heat oil in a frypan and cook the steak on fairly high temperature, turning every 30 seconds to ensure the juices are not forced to the surface. After 4 minutes, remove from the heat and allow to rest. Slice the meat finely with the grain into 1 cm (⅓ in) thick pieces. Set aside.
- Heat olive oil in a frypan. Add shallots and cook stirring occasionally, about 15 minutes. Transfer shallots to a sieve and drain.
- Heat a frypan and add the cashews. Keep turning so they brown a little without burning. Remove from heat.
- Add the finely-sliced steak to the salad. Add the dressing and toss to combine.
- Serve on a platter with toasted cashews and fried shallots.

Note: The dressing can be kept in the refrigerator for at least a month.

ANGUS BEEF SIRLOIN AND POTATO GRATIN WITH POACHED PRAWNS

The centre piece of this dish is the potato gratin. It would be worth investing in a mandolin-style slicer to finely slice the potatoes for this recipe. This is a dish that can be prepared the day before you require it.

Serves 4
Preparation time: 1½ hours

POTATO GRATIN

300 ml (10 fl oz) cream
pinch of salt
sprig fresh thyme (or tarragon)
1 tablespoon garlic, crushed
1½ kg (52 oz) Agria potatoes (or Yukon Golds), peeled and finely sliced
500 g (17½ oz) green beans, topped & tailed
220 ml (7 fl oz) fish stock
250 g (8½ oz) prawns (shrimp), deveined, tail intact
ice cubes
200 g (7 oz) beetroot, peeled
200 g (7 oz) radishes, washed
Citrus Vinaigrette (p. 136)
pinch of salt
1–2 tablespoons olive oil
1 kg (35 oz) sirloin steak, cut into 4 thick pieces
salt and pepper
handful pea feathers (tendrils), to garnish

METHOD

- Preheat oven to 150°C (300°F).
- Season the cream by heating in a pot adding salt until slightly over-salted.
- Infuse the cream with thyme and garlic stirring occasionally on a low heat.
- Layer the sliced potatoes in a greased baking dish lined with baking paper as carefully as possible since it will affect the finished product.
- Pour the cream over the potatoes and discard the thyme.
- Bake in the oven for 1 hour and then remove – a knife should slide easily through the potato when cooked. Allow to cool. If you are preparing this in advance, then refrigerate overnight. Reheat in a pre-heated oven at 180°C (350°F) until the surface is crisp. Remove and set aside.
- Blanch the green beans for 2 minutes in a pot of boiling water. Remove from heat, discard the water and refresh the beans in a bowl of icy or chilled water. Heat the fish stock in a pot until boiling and add the prawns to poach until just cooked. Remove from the heat and drain off the stock (freeze stock for use later if you wish). Refresh the prawns in a bowl of ice cubes.
- Finely slice the beetroot and radishes (with a mandolin/ slicer if you have one). Toss all the ingredients in the vinaigrette.
- Season the steak with salt and pepper. Add oil to a heavy skillet on high heat. Add the steak, cook on one side, then turn and cook on the other to ensure the juices are

retained. Depending on how rare you prefer your meat, cook for more or less time. Allow to rest for a couple of minutes.

- To serve, cut the potato gratin into serving sized squares. Drizzle the plates lightly with citrus vinaigrette and place potato gratin on each. Place the steak alongside the potato gratin and top with a generous serve of the vegetables in vinaigrette and a couple of well-placed prawns. Season with a pinch of salt and garnish with pea feathers.

PORK AND RABBIT RILLETTE

Lloyd first sampled a dish similar to this at a restaurant in Moncleuse, Provence. It was presented with a French onion marmalade to temper the richness of the rillette (a pâté).

Serves 4
Preparation time: 4 hours

INGREDIENTS

500 g (17½ oz) fatty pork belly
1 whole rabbit, jointed with bones in
6 whole garlic cloves
3 bay leaves
4 sprigs thyme
500 ml (16 fl oz) water or chicken stock
sea salt and freshly ground black
   pepper
cornichons (small pickled gherkins), to
   serve
crostini, store bought, to serve

METHOD

· Heat the oven to 160°C (325°F).
· Place the pork and rabbit in a baking dish together with the other ingredients. Cover with foil making sure the dish is sealed completely. Cook for 3 hours until the meat is completely tender. Remove from oven and take the meat out of the liquor (do not throw liquor away).
· Using a fork, shred the pork and remove all the meat from the bones of the rabbit. Season lightly with salt and pepper.
· Pack the meat mix into a 1 L (32 fl oz) glass preserving jar and pour the liquor in to cover and to create a seal of fat on top. Refrigerate until set.
· Serve the rillette with cornichons and crostini.

GOAT CURRY

When Lloyd first purchased Highgate Hill farm there was 2500 acres (1011 hectares) of land with many wild goats grazing on it. Despite having a pet goat of their own (who liked to be indoors), Lloyd cooked a goat dish for the first time. This recipe is dedicated to Krusty, their pet goat.

Serves 6
Preparation time: 2 hours

INGREDIENTS

2 tablespoons olive oil
2 pinches salt
600 g (1 lb 5 oz) goat meat, deboned, trimmed and cubed
2 onions
4 large tomatoes
6 cloves garlic
2½ cm (2 in) ginger root
2 red chillies
large bunch coriander (cilantro), roots and stems
2 teaspoons coriander seeds
2 teaspoons cumin seeds
2 teaspoons fennel seeds
2 teaspoons yellow mustard seeds
2 teaspoons black mustard seeds
1 teaspoon cardamom seeds (or 10–15 cardamom pods)
½ teaspoon cloves
3 cinnamon quills
2 teaspoons turmeric
2 teaspoons garam masala
1 teaspoon cumin powder
4 teaspoons hot curry powder
300 ml (10 fl oz) water
1 large potato (or 2 medium-sized)
2 teaspoons green herb stock
750 gm (26½ oz) rice

METHOD

- Pour two tablespoons of oil into a large pot and heat until hot. Sprinkle two pinches of salt into the oil. Add the goat meat to the pot turning each piece until brown. Remove from the pot and place in a separate dish to cool.
- Peel and quarter the onions and tomatoes. Peel and slice the garlic and ginger and chop the chillies, removing the seeds if you prefer a milder curry.
- Clean the roots of the coriander, cutting the stems away from the leaves.
- Add the coriander seeds, cumin and fennel seeds to a mortar and pestle and crush, making sure they are well ground. Add powder together with the mustard seeds and re-heat the hot oil, ensuring there is a lid on the pot.
- Once the mustard seeds begin to pop, add the roots and stems of the coriander, the chillies, cardamom seeds or pods, cloves, garlic, ginger, onions, cinnamon quills, a teaspoon of salt and tomatoes and fry together on a high heat.
- Cook until the onion is golden and soft, stirring frequently to ensure nothing sticks to the bottom of the pot.
- Add the browned meat, turmeric, garam masala, cumin powder, curry powder and cook for another 5 minutes on a continuously high heat stirring occasionally.
- Cover with water and simmer on a low heat for 1½ hours stirring occasionally. Add more water if required (but this is more of a dry curry to be eaten with rice).
- Peel and cube the potatoes and add to the curry together with the green herb stock. Ensure the potatoes

TO SERVE
500 g (17½ oz) basmati rice (cooked to
   packet instructions)
small bunch coriander (cilantro) leaves
1 lemon, juice
roti, store bought
lime pickle, store bought

are well covered and cook for a further 30 minutes.
- Remove from heat.
- To serve, add rice to the bowls, ladle in the goat curry
  and garnish with coriander leaves and a squeeze a lemon.
- Serve with roti and lime pickle.

CRUMBED VEAL WITH APPLE SLAW AND MACADAMIA NUTS

Lloyd first tried this in Vienna when he was very young and loved it. It's an ideal lunchtime dish that will appeal to the whole family. If you prefer an alternative to veal, it can be substituted for thinly sliced skinless chicken breast.

Serves 6
Preparation time: 1 hour

CRUMBED VEAL

2 tablespoons plain (all-purpose) flour
salt and pepper
3–4 free range eggs, lightly beaten
600 g (19 oz) veal, very thinly sliced
panko crumbs, store bought
light olive oil, for frying

APPLE SLAW

1 large carrot, thinly sliced
1 crisp green apple, thinly sliced
1 fennel bulb, thinly sliced
½ a red cabbage, thinly sliced
small bunch chives, chopped
3 tablespoons Citrus Vinaigrette, (p. 136)
sea salt and freshly ground pepper

BEURRE NOISETTE

2 tablespoon salted butter, cubed
½ lemon, juice
2 tablespoons roasted macadamia nuts, chopped

METHOD

- Place the flour on a shallow dish and season. Lightly beat the eggs in a bowl and place the panko crumbs on a plate.
- Crumb each piece of veal by dipping in the seasoned flour, then coat with the eggs and roll in panko crumbs. Refrigerate the crumbed veal while you prepare the salad.
- Mix together sliced carrot, apple, fennel and red cabbage. Add the chives, vinaigrette and season to taste.
- To cook the veal, heat the pan with oil on a moderate to high temperature and add crumbed veal. After 1–2 minutes turn and cook for a further minute until each side is a light brown colour and the veal is cooked medium rare.
- To make the beurre noisette, add the butter to a hot saucepan. Reduce heat when the butter starts to brown. Mix in the lemon juice and add the macadamia nuts.
- Remove the pan from the heat.
- Place the crumbed veal on plates with a spoonful of the beurre noisette over the crumbed veal. Serve with the slaw on the side.

Note: Beurre noisette is French for any type of butter sauce where the butter has been cooked until golden or nut brown. It can be flavoured with different herbs and spices.

CHICKEN BREAST WITH COUSCOUS, FETA AND DUKKAH

A classic chicken dish reminiscent of travels to Morocco, the sweet flavours of chicken and mascapone work superbly alongside the spice and tanginess of dukkah and feta.

Serves 6
Preparation time: 2 hours

INGREDIENTS

6 chicken breasts, 1 kg (2 lb)
sea salt and freshly ground black
  pepper
120 g (4½ oz) couscous, cooked
100 g (3½oz) Danish feta
35 g (1½ oz) Dukkah (p. 76)
45 g (2 oz) garlic cloves, roasted
20 g (1 oz) mascarpone
10 g (½ oz) flat leaf parsley, chopped
Ratatouille (p. 82), to serve

METHOD

- Lay the chicken breast skin side down. Use a paring knife to create a pocket by slicing horizontally across the middle through the thickest part of the breast being careful not to disconnect from the skin. Season the inside of the chicken breast very generously with sea salt and freshly ground black pepper. Set aside.
- To make the stuffing, combine cooked couscous, feta, dukkah, garlic cloves, mascarpone and chopped parsley. Divide the mixture into six even portions of about 50 g (2 oz) each. Place a portion of stuffing into the pocket you have made in the chicken breast, fold it from the thick end and roll the chicken breast tightly in glad wrap. Refrigerate for at least an hour or if possible the day before is best.
- Pre-heat the oven to 180°C (350°F).
- Remove glad wrap from the chicken breast and heat a pan to medium heat, cooking each side of the chicken breast to seal the outside. Place them in an oven dish, skin side up to ensure the pocket stays intact. Cook for 20–30 mins or until the juice runs clear. Check the core temperature using a meat thermometer 74°C (165°F).
- Slice the chicken and serve with ratatouille.

Note: Uncooked stuffed chicken is better left overnight in the refrigerator.

DUCK CASSOULET

This dish, originating from southern France, is made traditionally with pork sausage, goose, duck and white haricot beans in a tomato-based sauce. At The Cove, it is served with confit of duck. It is important to make the duck leg confit the day before. The cassoulet stock needs to simmer for at least three to four hours before you need it and can be made a day ahead of time too. When creating your own cassoulet, it pays to invest in good-quality, aged meat.

Serves 4–6
Preparation time: 1½ hours + 1 day

DUCK LEG CONFIT

220–250 g (7–9 oz) duck legs
1 tablespoon sea salt
½ teaspoon ground pepper
4 cloves garlic, smashed
4 sprigs thyme
1 tablespoon duck fat (or olive oil)

CASSOULET

2 medium bacon hocks
2 carrots, roughly chopped
2 onions, 1 roughly chopped, 1 finely diced
2 stalks celery, roughly chopped
2 sprigs thyme
1 L (35 fl oz) water
1 kg (2 lb 3 oz) white beans, soaked overnight in cold water
1 tablespoon duck fat (or olive oil)
1 teaspoon thyme leaves, chopped
1 teaspoon rosemary, chopped
1 tablespoon garlic, chopped
250 g (9 oz) streaky bacon, chopped
250 g (9 oz) smoked sausage, good quality
125 ml (4 fl oz) tomato paste

METHOD

- To prepare the duck leg confit, place duck legs in a large bowl and rub salt, pepper, garlic and thyme into the skin. Place in an airtight container and refrigerate for 24 hours.
- Remove the duck, brush off any excess seasoning and place legs snugly in a baking dish. Cover with duck fat and cook at 100°C (225°F) for 2½ hours until legs are completely tender.
- Once cooked, remove from heat and allow the duck legs to cool in the fat. Remove the fat and bake duck legs in a hot oven 220°C (425°F) until crisp, about 10 minutes.
- To make the cassoulet stock, cook bacon hocks with carrots, roughly chopped onion, celery and thyme sprigs in water. Bring to the boil and then simmer for 3–4 hours until the meat has come away from the bone.
- Remove the meat and strain the stock through a sieve. Reserve the stock.
- Drain the beans and add to the reserved stock. Bring to the boil then reduce to a simmer and cook until tender, being careful not to overcook. Drain the beans and set aside.
- In a heavy-based pot, add duck fat and fry the finely diced onion, chopped rosemary and a teaspoon of thyme in a tablespoon of duck fat or 100 ml (3½ fl oz) of olive oil. Add the chopped streaky bacon and cook until the fat is rendered and slightly browned.

1 L (35 fl oz) tomato juice
1 tablespoon wholegrain mustard

FENNEL PURÉE

250 g (9 oz) fennel bulb, finely sliced
50 g (2 oz) salted butter
1 clove garlic
salt and pepper, to taste
100 ml (3½ fl oz) cream

CARAMELISED ONION

4 tablespoons duck fat (or olive oil)
1 kg (2 lb 3 oz) white onions
2 teaspoons sugar
salt and pepper, to taste
2 bay leaves
3 sprigs thyme
2 tablespoons red wine vinegar

TO SERVE

parsley (or rosemary) leaves, to garnish
fresh bread, toasted
cornishons
hot mustard of choice

- Combine the sliced sausage and tomato paste and continue cooking for 3 minutes, stirring occasionally. Add the tomato juice, cooked white beans and the cooked hock. Stir in the mustard until the mixture is thickened. Set aside.
- To make the fennel purée, place the finely sliced fennel with butter and garlic in a heavy frypan to melt. Add salt and pepper. Fry on a moderate heat until the fennel is completely cooked through. Add the cream and bring to the boil stirring occasionally. Remove from heat, place contents in a blender and purée until smooth.
- To make the caramelised onion, melt the duck fat in a heavy-based pot on a medium heat. Add sliced onions and coat in the fat. Sprinkle in sugar, salt and pepper and continue to stir ensuring the onions do not brown in colour.
- Add bay leaves and sprigs of thyme. Increase the heat and stir continuously, ensuring the onions don't stick. Continue cooking until the onions colour to a golden brown, then add red wine vinegar. Stir and remove from heat.
- Select a large wooden board or platter to serve this dish. Ladle a dollop of fennel purée and place the sausages in the centre. Add the duck leg with a small ramekin of caramelised onion. Put the warm bean cassoulet in a separate dish on the board. Add parsley or rosemary frond to garnish. Served with freshly baked bread, cornichons and a hot grain mustard.

Note: Duck fat can be refrigerated and re-used.

SUGAR CURED BEEF WITH CORIANDER PESTO

This dish has fresh, sweet and savoury flavours. It will need to be prepared 48 hours before serving.

Serves 4–6
Preparation time: 30 minutes (+ 48 hours prep time for cured beef)

THE BEEF
500 g (17½ oz) eye fillet beef
1 tablespoon thyme, chopped
100 g (3½ oz) peppercorns (black,
  white, and Szechuan), crushed
150 g (5 oz) caster (superfine) sugar
250 g (9 oz) rock salt
60 ml (2 fl oz) brandy

SALAD
green beans, 100 g (3½ oz) per person
18 semi-dried tomatoes
1–2 tablespoons Pickled Red Onions,
  (p. 137)
1 tablespoon Coriander Pesto, (p. 143)
drizzle of olive oil

METHOD
- Remove any fat and silver skin from the beef to allow the flavours from the marinade to fully soak into the beef.
- Roll the beef in the chopped thyme and crushed peppercorns.
- Add caster sugar, rock salt and brandy to cover the beef.
- Cover the dish and place in the refrigerator. Turn the beef every 6 hours for 48 hours.
- To make the salad, blanch the green beans and toss together with the semi-dried tomatoes, pickled red onions, coriander pesto and black olive oil to taste. Thinly slice the beef and serve with the salad.

LAMB RAGOUT WITH ITALIAN SWEET AND SOUR SAUCE AND BAKED SAFFRON POLENTA

This is an all time favourite weekend winter dish. Don't be put off by the various preparations involved in this recipe, as the polenta and the sweet and sour sauce can be made in advance.

Serves 4–6
Preparation time: 4 hours

BRAISED LAMB

2 kg (4 lb) lamb shoulder
olive oil
sea salt and pepper
1 onion, roughly chopped
1 carrot, roughly chopped
2 stalks celery, roughly chopped
½ leek, roughly chopped
1 tablespoon chopped garlic
2 tablespoons tomato paste
2 sprigs thyme
2 sprigs rosemary
1½ L (3 pt fl oz) chicken or lamb stock
600 g (24 oz) spinach, wilted

ITALIAN SWEET AND SOUR SAUCE

50 g (2 oz) butter
50 g (2 oz) plain (all purpose) flour
1 tablespoon olive oil
1 onion, diced
1 carrot, diced
2 stalks celery, diced
2 teaspoons garlic, crushed
75 ml (2½ fl oz) balsamic vinegar

METHOD

- Preheat oven to 150°C (300°F). Lightly oil and season the lamb with salt and pepper. In a hot frypan, seal and brown both sides of the lamb. Move the meat to a deep baking/braising dish and put aside.
- Using the same frypan, add onion, carrot, celery and leek. Cook until soft (the onion should be translucent, not brown) being careful not to over fry them. Add garlic, tomato paste, thyme and rosemary and cook for a couple of minutes until the sauce bubbles.
- Add the sauce to the lamb. Pour in the chicken or lamb stock, ensuring the meat is completely submerged. Cover the dish with baking paper and seal tightly with tin foil.
- Bake for approximately 2–2½ hours. Check a knife can pass through the meat with relative ease, then remove from the oven and leave covered in the braising liquid to keep the meat tender and moist.
- To make a roux for the Italian sweet and sour sauce, melt butter in a saucepan, then add flour and stir over a low heat until the mixture is a light golden colour. Transfer to a separate bowl. Add olive oil to the same saucepan or a frypan, add the onion, carrot and celery and gently cook until onion is translucent. Add the garlic and the roux. Once completely mixed, add the balsamic vinegar, red currant jelly, tomato sauce, lemon and orange zest, raisins and toasted pine nuts. Simmer gently and then add the lamb braising liquid. Season with salt and pepper to your preference.

100 ml (3½ fl oz) red current jelly
4 tablespoons tomato sauce (ketchup)
zest of 1 lemon
zest of ½ orange
75 g (3 oz) raisins
75 g (3 oz) pinenuts, toasted
1¼ L (42 fl oz) lamb braising liquid,
   reduced

BAKED SAFFRON POLENTA
500 ml (16 fl oz) water
100 g (3½ oz) salted butter
Garlic Confit (p. 140)
1 teaspoon saffron threads
300 g (10½ oz) polenta
60 g (2½ oz) Parmesan cheese

- To prepare the baked saffron polenta, pre-heat oven to 180C (350F) combine water, butter, garlic confit and saffron in a pan and bring to the boil. Gradually add the polenta and grated Parmesan, cooking on a gentle heat and stirring continuously. When the mixture comes away from the side of the pan without being tacky to the touch, remove from the heat and mould so that it is 1 cm (in) thick on a tray lined with baking paper. Leave to cool completely, then cut into rectangles. Bake the polenta until golden, about 15 minutes.
- Note: This method of cooking the lamb also works well for lamb shanks and beef cheeks. The braising liquid is best left in the refrigerator overnight so the fat settles on top. Remove the fat off the lamb, leaving the remaining braising liquid. You can deep fry the polenta if you prefer for about 10 minutes until golden.
- Serve the lamb lightly drizzled with sweet and sour sauce. Add wilted spinach and polenta to accompany the dish.

ROASTED HIGHGATE HILL LAMB

Although this is essentially a summer salad, the ingredients are interchangeable depending on the season. Quinoa is available in several different colours and any of them can be used for this recipe. Romesco salsa originates from the north east of Spain and is made from various nuts, red capsicums (bell peppers) and roasted garlic. Dukkah is an Egyptian condiment designed to literally spice up a meal.

Serves 4–6
Preparation time: 1 hour

ROMESCO SALSA

5 large tomatoes
125 ml (4 fl oz) olive oil
38 g (1½ oz) whole almonds
1 tablespoon garlic, crushed
75 g (3 oz) capsicum (red bell peppers), roasted
2 teaspoons smoked paprika
½ teaspoon chilli flakes
50 ml (2 fl oz) red wine vinegar

DUKKAH

50 g (2 oz) hazelnuts
50 g (2oz) almonds
50 g (2 oz) pistachio
50 g (2 oz) sesame seeds
2 tablespoons coriander seeds
2 tablespoons cumin seeds
1 teaspoon sea salt
1 teaspoon black pepper
1 teaspoon sumac

250 g (8 oz) quinoa
500 ml (16 fl oz) water
2–3 lamb racks (allow 3 rib chops per person)
salt and pepper

METHOD

- Preheat the oven to 180°C (350°F).
- To make the romesco salsa, put the tomatoes, olive oil, almonds, garlic and red peppers into a pan and roast in the oven until tomatoes are tender. Remove for the pan and when cool, place in a kitchen blender. Add the smoked paprika, chilli flakes, red wine vinegar and blend until smooth. Season and set aside.
- To make the dukkah, dry toast the nuts separately in a frypan over medium heat. Once cool, combine the nuts and spices in a food processor and blend ingredients together.
- To cook the quinoa, rinse in a sieve under cold running water to remove the bitter flavour. Place in a saucepan with the water and bring to the boil then cover and turn to simmer until most of the liquid is absorbed. Remove from heat and allow to stand for 10–15 minutes. Set aside until serving.
- Season the lamb well with salt and cracked pepper. Add oil to a hot pan, add the lamb and seal, reducing any large amounts of fat by leaving fat side down on a medium heat to caramelise.
- Put the lamb into the pre-heated oven and cook until medium rare or longer depending on your preference, about 15 minutes for medium rare. Rest for at least 10 minutes before serving.
- To serve, make a pillow of quinoa on each plate. Carve

1 tablespoon preserved lemon peel,
  finely diced
3 tomatoes
2 red capsicums (bell peppers)
2 green capsicums (bell peppers)
2 yellow capsicums (bell peppers)
1 corn cob
1 avocado
1 bulb fennel
Citrus Vinaigrette (p. 136), to taste
salt and pepper, to taste
pita bread (optional)

the lamb chops, and place 3 on each plate. Top with Romesco salsa and a sprinkle of dukkah. You can serve additional dukkah on the side with pita bread if using.

- Note: The salsa can be served warm or cold and stored in the refrigerator for up to one week. Dukkah is best kept in a cool place.

PORK BELLY WITH ROASTED PARSNIPS AND SALSA VERDE

Lloyd first tried pork belly served with a wholegrain mustard potato mash at gastro-pub, The Engineer, in London. He loved it so much, he decided to add it to the menu at The Cove.

Serves 4–6
Preparation time: 30 minutes

SALSA VERDE
100 g (3½ oz) parsley, chopped
100 g (3½ oz) basil leaves, chopped
100 g (3½ oz) tarragon, chopped
100 g (3½ oz) chives, chopped
1 tablespoon capers, chopped
1 tablespoon cornichons, chopped
½ tablespoon spring onions (scallions), chopped
1 clove garlic, chopped
125 ml (4 fl oz) olive oil
2 tablespoons of red wine vinegar
salt and pepper
1 head broccoli, cut into florets

ROASTED PARSNIPS
1 kg (2 lb) parsnips, peeled, quartered
salt and pepper
1 tablespoon olive oil

PORK BELLY
2 kg (4 lb) pork belly
salt and pepper
1 tablespoon fennel seeds
3 tablespoons olive oil
Fennel Purée (p. 72), to serve

METHOD
- To make the salsa verde, combine ingredients together and toss. Set aside.
- Preheat oven to 180°C (350°F).
- To roast parsnips, season with salt and pepper and coat with olive oil.
- Place on a greased baking tray lined with baking paper. Bake in the oven until crisp on the outside, but still tender on the inside, about 25 minutes.
- Preheat oven to 160°C (325°F).
- Score the skin of the pork belly. Season liberally with salt and pepper and coat with the fennel seeds.
- Place oil in a deep baking dish, add pork belly and cover with tin foil.
- Bake for 2–3 hours until the belly is tender. When cooked, a knife should pass through the meat easily. Leave the meat to rest in the tray for about 10 minutes.
- Steam broccoli florets in a pot of boiling water for five minutes, drain and set aside.
- To serve, slice the pork belly and add to each plate with parsnips. Ladle over a generous serve of salse verde. Add broccoli florets.

VENISON WITH POTATO ALSACE

There are plenty of wild deer at Highgate hill and Lloyd took the opportunity to cook venison, trying various different cuts. The back straps and tenderloins are best for flash frying and are recommended for this particular dish. The juniper berries complement the venison and the potato Alsace, coated in Swiss cheese and layered with garlic, makes it a country-style dish.

Serves 4–6
Preparation time: 45 minutes

POTATO ALSACE

8–10 large baking potatoes (high starch are best)
400 g (14 oz) Swiss (or Jarlsberg) cheese, sliced
10–12 garlic cloves, crushed
salt and pepper
500–750 ml (16–24 fl oz) cream

VENISON

8–10 juniper berries
handful fresh thyme leaves
sea salt and black pepper
2 knobs butter
1 kg (2 lb) venison tenderloin
1 tablespoon olive oil

THE JUS

1 large onion
2 knobs butter
175 ml (6 fl oz) port
175 ml (6 fl oz) red wine
2 bay leaves
6–10 juniper berries
500 ml (16 fl oz) beef stock
salt, to taste

METHOD

- Preheat oven to 180°C (350°F).
- Peel the potatoes. Slice finely (a mandolin helps) then wash thoroughly to remove excess starch. Pat the potato slices dry and set aside.
- Line a baking dish with baking paper and place the sliced potatoes as neatly as possible to create a base layer. Cover the layer with slices of Swiss cheese, some of the garlic and a sprinkle of salt and pepper.
- Repeat process as many times as the depth of the baking dish will allow.
- Pour the cream over until it almost covers the top of the potato layers.
- Place in the oven and cook for 90 minutes or until the potatoes are soft and the cream has been absorbed.
- Remove from heat and serve straight away or allow to cool and refrigerate.
- To make the jus, pan fry the onion in one knob of butter until the onion caramelises. Add port, red wine, bay leaves and the juniper berries and cook until the liquid reduces by half. Add beef stock and continue to cook. Add the second knob of butter stirring for a minute. Remove from heat, remove the bay leaves and set aside.
- To prepare the venison, in a mortar and pestle, crush together the juniper berries and thyme with a pinch of salt and pepper. Smear two knobs of butter over the venison and pour the berry and thyme mix over the loin to cover completely. Coat in glad wrap and allow to rest for 30 minutes.
- Heat a heavy-based frypan or skillet and add a tablespoon of olive oil. Slice the loin, preferably 2–3 cm (¾–1 in) thick depending on how rare you like it, and sear in hot oil for two minutes turning to brown each side.
- Once cooked, remove from the heat and allow to rest for a few minutes.
- To serve, place the venison on plates and pour over the jus. Serve with potato Alsace.

Note: The venison is best cooked medium rare.

RATATOUILLE

This versatile recipe can be used with lamb, beef or fish. It also makes a great accompaniment to gnocchi (p. 87).

Serves 6
Preparation time: 40 minutes

INGREDIENTS
1 red onion, diced
2 tablespoons garlic
1 tablespoon rosemary leaves, finely
  chopped
125 ml (14 fl oz) olive oil
4 capsicums, assorted colours
2 eggplants (aubergines), cubed
4 zucchini (courgettes), cut into small
  cubes
2 tablespoons tomato paste
1¼ L (42 fl oz) tomato juice
2 tablespoons basil leaves, chopped
salt and pepper

METHOD
- In a heavy-based pot, combine onion, garlic, rosemary and olive oil on a low heat. Cook until the onions are soft. Add the chopped capsicums, eggplant, zucchini and tomato paste. Simmer until the vegetables begin to soften.
- Add the tomato juice and basil. Season to taste with salt and pepper.
- Serve with your favourite fish, beef or lamb dish or as is with a green salad of choice.

Note: The key to a good ratatouille is cooking the vegetables sufficiently for flavour, without completely stewing them. Ratatouille can be eaten hot or cold.

Livy from Glencairn Garden Centre supplies micro greens and chillies for both restaurants.

BAKED POTATO GNOCCHI WITH MUSHROOM DUXELLE

This dish is a mainstay at The Cove. We use mushroom duxelle, a finely-chopped blend of white or brown mushrooms. You can use any blend, but for more flavour, add wild porcini mushrooms.

Serves 6–8 depending if entrée or main
Preparation time: 2 hours

MUSHROOM DUXELLE
600 g (21 oz) white and brown mushrooms
2 tablespoons olive oil

GNOCCHI
1.3 kg (45½ oz) Agria potatoes, dry mashed
50 g (2 oz) Parmesan, shaved
2 eggs, lightly beaten
300 g (10½ oz) tempura flour (or tempura batter mix)
knob of salted butter

GARNISH
Napolitano Sauce, (p. 92)
250 g (9 oz) baby spinach leaves, wilted
2–3 bunches broccoli, steamed
18 small tomatoes, semi roasted
6 large Portobello (field) mushrooms
200 g (7 oz) goats' cheese
4 teaspoons olive oil (or Basil Pesto (p. 143), to drizzle
handful of fresh basil leaves, to garnish

METHOD
- To make the mushroom duxelle, finely chop the mushrooms by hand or in a food processor. Sauté in a pan at a low heat until all the moisture evaporates and you are left with a dry mushroom mix strong in flavour.
- To make the gnocchi, preheat oven to 250°C (500°F).
- Boil the potatoes until completely cooked through, then drain until all the moisture is removed. Once potatoes have cooled, mash until the texture is dry and crumbly. Add the Parmesan, beaten eggs and mushroom duxelle and stir to combine. Add tempura flour and work through until you have a smooth dough.
- Sprinkle flour on a clean board or bench top. Take a quarter of the dough and using the tips of your fingers roll the dough gently out from the centre. Once you have about 30 cm (12 in) in length, cut into 2 cm (¾ in) pieces, and place on a tray lined with parchment paper. Repeat the process with the remaining dough.
- Place the gnocchi on non-stick oven tray (about 7 per person) and bake at for approximately 12 minutes, turning the pieces over at 8 minutes.
- Cut mushrooms in half and lightly saute in a pan at a medium to high heat. Set aside.
- Once the gnocchi are golden in colour and light and fluffy, remove from the oven and add a knob of salted butter to coat.
- To serve, place gnocchi on plates, drizzle with Napolitano sauce. Add wilted spinach, broccoli, tomatoes and mushrooms. Crumble goats' cheese over and pour olive oil around the plates to finish.

SPINACH AND RICOTTA GNOCCHI WITH BRAISED BEEF CHEEK AND PORTOBELLO MUSHROOM

This dish has remained on the restaurant menu since The Cove opened. It's a popular choice largely because the gnocchi is so light and the texture and flavour combinations work wonderfully alongside the beef cheeks.

Serves 4–6
Preparation time: 45 minutes

BRAISED BEEF CHEEKS

2 kg (4 lb) beef cheeks, excess fat trimmed
salt and pepper
4 tablespoons olive oil (or more if required)
1 onion, chopped
1 carrot, chopped
2 stalks celery
1 tablespoon garlic, chopped
2 tablespoons tomato paste
250 ml (8 fl oz) red wine
2 L (4 pt) beef stock (or water)
2 sprigs thyme
2 tablespoons grain mustard
2 tablespoons tarragon, chopped
2 tablespoons flat leaf parsley

GNOCCHI

500 g (17½ oz) baby spinach leaves
2 eggs
80 g (3 oz) Parmesan, shaved
½ tablespoon Basil Pesto (p. 143)
500 g (17 ½ oz) Ricotta cheese
175 g (6 oz) tempura flour (or tempura batter mix)

METHOD

- To cook the beef cheeks, preheat oven to 160°C (325°F).
- Season beef cheeks with salt and pepper. Heat a frypan with 4 tablespoons of olive oil, add the beef cheeks and thoroughly seal until both sides of the meat are brown. Transfer to a deep baking or roasting dish.
- Add onion, carrot, celery and garlic to the same pan used to seal the beef (with extra olive oil if required) and cook, stirring occasionally, for five minutes. Transfer to the roasting dish. Add tomato paste, red wine, beef stock, rosemary and thyme to the pan, ensuring the meat is submerged. Seal the dish with tin foil and bake in the oven for 3–4 hours. If you can pass a knife through the meat with very little pressure, it is ready.
- Leave for two hours covered with the foil to cool in its juices.
- Remove meat from the liquor. Set the liquor aside to use for mushroom ragout later.
- Add grain mustard, tarragon and parsley to the meat. Season with salt and pepper to taste.
- Press or roll the meat, wrap in cling film and refrigerate. Remove from the refrigerator, discard cling film and cut the meat to desired portion size. Reheat in the oven on a moderate temperature just before you require it, ensuring the meat doesn't dry out.
- To make the gnocchi, preheat oven to 250°C (500°F).
- In a saucepan of boiling water, blanch the spinach leaves and once wilted cool quickly and squeeze out excess moisture.
- Add eggs, Parmesan, basil pesto and blanched spinach to a food processor and blend until completely smooth. Remove

MUSHROOM RAGOUT

50 g (2 oz) dry porcini mushrooms
2 tablespoons olive oil
1 small white onion, finely diced
2 teaspoons garlic
500 g (17½ oz) Portobello (field)
  mushrooms
sea salt and black pepper
250 ml (8 fl oz) beef stock (from
  the beef cheeks)
1 teaspoon rosemary, chopped
1 teaspoon thyme, chopped

TO GARNISH

extra Ricotta cheese
8–12 cherry tomatoes
micro salad greens

from the mixer into a bowl and fold in the Ricotta (drained overnight if necessary) and the tempura flour. Combine and refrigerate for one hour.

- Sprinkle flour on a clean board or bench top. Take ¼ of the dough and using the tips of your fingers roll the dough gently out from the centre. Once you have about 30 cm (12 in) in length, cut into 2 cm (¾ in) pieces, and place on a tray lined with parchment paper. Repeat the process with the remaining dough.
- To cook the gnocchi, place about 7 pieces per person on non-stick oven tray and bake for approximately 12 minutes, turning the pieces over at 8 minutes. Once the gnocchi are golden in colour and light and fluffy, remove from oven and add a knob of salted butter to coat the gnocchi. Cover and set aside.
- To make the mushroom ragout, soak the Porcini mushrooms in water for five minutes to soften. Drain and dry well then set aside.
- Add the olive oil to a medium hot frypan. Add the onion and cook until soft and translucent (but not brown). Add garlic and cook for a further minute.
- Add the mushrooms, sea salt and freshly ground black pepper to the onions.
- Add beef stock and cook through on moderate heat.
- To serve, portion a generous ladle of ragout. Add gnocchi, top with the beef cheek, and garnish with dobs of extra Ricotta, halved cherry tomatoes and micro greens.

Note: The meat portion of this dish will need to be prepared a few hours before you plan to serve it. For this recipe you need only about 7–8 gnocchi per person. Any spare gnocchi can be frozen and kept for 2–3 weeks.

SICILIAN PASTA SAUCE

An original Sicilian tomato sauce using fresh herbs is ideal for use in pastas, pizzas, and for serving with meatballs or seafood.

Serves 6
Preparation time: 40 minutes

INGREDIENTS
3 tablespoons olive oil
1 onion, diced
1 tablespoon garlic, crushed
1 teaspoon dried chilli, crushed
2 teaspoons thyme, chopped
1 tablespoon tomato paste
1 kg (2 lb) tomatoes (or canned whole, peeled), chopped
150 g (5 oz) mixed olives, chopped
50 g (2 oz) capers, chopped
2 anchovies, chopped

METHOD
- Add olive oil to a frypan over medium heat. Add onion, garlic, dried chilli, thyme and cook until the onions are soft and translucent.
- Add tomato paste, tomatoes and simmer for a few minutes. Mix in the olives, capers and anchovies. Simmer on a low heat for 5 minutes. Remove from heat and allow to cool.

Note: When you are ready to serve, mix the sauce with freshly chopped parsley. Any excess can be kept refrigerated or frozen in a glass container.

ITALIAN-STYLE PIZZA

Pizzas are a mainstay at The Cove and The Quay restuarants, so ensuring we have the right base and a tasty pizza sauce is important. Given the preparation time, it's a good idea to double the recipe (for dough and sauce) and freeze what you don't require for another time.

Serves 4–6
Preparation time: 2 hours (+ 2½ hours for dough to rise)

DOUGH
1⅘ kg (64⅓ oz) flour
50 g (1¾ oz) table salt
1 teaspoon instant dried yeast
1 L (32 fl oz) water, room temperature
75 ml (2 fl oz) olive oil

NAPOLITANO SAUCE
50 ml (1¾ fl oz) olive oil
70 g (2⅓ oz) butter
250 g (9 oz) onions, diced
150 g (5 oz) celery, diced
1 tablespoon garlic, crushed
1 kg (2 lb) peeled tomatoes chopped,
750 g (26½ oz) tomato paste
75 g (2½ oz) Parmesan, grated
2½ teaspoons basil
2½ teaspoons dried oregano
1 teaspoon ground black pepper
1 tablespoon fennel seeds
pinch of salt
2½ teaspoons sugar

SIMPLE TOPPING SUGGESTIONS
basil and tomato slices
olives, anchovies and capers
salmon and asparagus
potatoes, cubed
Mozzarella cheese (or cheese of
    choice), grated or sliced
Garlic Aioli (p. 142), optional, to drizzle

METHOD
- Preheat oven to 250°C (500°F).
- To make the pizza dough, mix the dry ingredients together, then add the water and olive oil into the dry ingredients. Knead the dough with your hands (or use a mixer) to work the dough to a smooth texture.
- Place the dough in a large bowl and cover with cling film, leaving it in a warm place for a minimum of 2 hours to double in size.
- While the dough is rising, make the sauce. Put olive oil, butter, onion, celery and crushed garlic in a heavy-based pot and cook on moderate heat until the vegetables are soft, about 15–20 minutes.
- Purée and return to pot. Add tomatoes, tomato paste, Parmesan, dried basil, dried oregano, ground black pepper, fennel seeds, bay leaves, salt, and sugar and simmer for 30 minutes. Set aside.
- Divide the dough into 300 g (10½ oz) portions and cover again, leaving in a warm place for a further hour.
- Roll the dough into 30–40 cm (12–14 in) discs then place on greased pizza trays).
- Coat the base in the pizza sauce and add a topping of your choice, finishing with a good sprinkling of cheese of choice. Place in the oven and cook for 7–10 minutes.
- Remove from oven, drizzle with garlic aioli and serve immediately with your favourite salad.

Note: As this recipe is designed for a large quantity of pizzas, you can freeze any unrisen dough for use at a later date.

Dan from Mangawhai Meat shop smokes meat for The Cove café.

Brewers Kirsty and Mike from the Leigh Sawmill Brewery supply craft beer to both restaurants.

COASTAL CATCH

*I'm used to juggling things. I've spent my whole life with several
pots on the boil.*
Lloyd

Drawn to the Bream Bay area, Lloyd dreamed he could create a successful business in the region. Putting his unique stamp on the coastal property, The Cove café soon became a reality.

He refashioned the interior of the café, gutting the old storage room to create a bright indoor dining space, alfresco deck and nautical bar that faces Waipu Cove and the beach.

Craig Estick was appointed Executive Chef and an innovative menu followed. The dishes combine Highgate produce with freshly-caught seafood. The fish specials change daily, but almost always have a South Pacific influence.

Although actively involved, Lloyd takes a hands-off approach in the kitchen, allowing Craig to be creatively unhindered.

'My experience in hospitality taught me that artistic people need their independence,' said Lloyd of his decision.

Pastry chef, Mikal Haakman, produces the café's cakes and sweets and assists sous chef, Lewis Oliver, in the main kitchen on busy weekends.

Lloyd's pet hate is waste and he applies that philosophy at the café.

'I won't throw anything away and I encourage the kitchen staff to use everything. Any excess food goes back to feed the pigs at the farm. It makes environmental sense.'

In an effort to support local industry, the restaurant sources as much as possible from the region. The micro greens and chillies are grown in Waipu at Glencairn Garden Centre, the cheeses are from the Cheese Shop in Kaiwaka, and the Highgate Hill meat is prepared and smoked at the Mangawhai Meat Shop.

The comprehensive wine list is well represented by various New Zealand labels, together with local Mangawhai favourite, Lochiel Estate Vineyard.

A smaller selection of French and Californian wines, together with boutique beer brewed locally at Leigh Sawmill Brewery, complements the beverage menu.

The Cove café has a busy vibe most weekends, with live music on Sunday afternoons in summer. Local surfies congregate for breakfast, and regulars with pet canines meet for coffee on the outdoor deck.

Michael describes his partner as a perfectionist who will do whatever it takes to get the job done.

'Lloyd loves people, and knowing his customers are having a great time with friends and family in his restaurants means everything to him. This is what drives him to ensure the food, the level of service, and the environment is the best it can be.'

STEAMED MUSSELS

Lloyd's interior design work took him on weekend trips to Paris. His biggest treat was gorging on mussels and French fries at his favourite café, Chez de Louisette in Paris.

Serves 4–6
Preparation time: 30 minutes

COMPOUND BUTTER

100 g (3½ oz) soft salted butter
1 teaspoon garlic, crushed
1 teaspoon ginger, grated
zest of 1 lemon
whole chilli, chopped

1 kg (35 oz) washed mussels
150 ml (5 fl oz) white wine
3 tablespoons flat leaf parsley leaves,
   chopped, to garnish
fresh crusty bread, to serve

METHOD

- Mix the compound butter ingredients together and roll into a cylinder in glad wrap. Refrigerate.
- Rinse and scrub the mussels under cold water and drain in a sieve to get rid of any debris or seaweed. Soak the mussels in a bowl of clean, cool water for 20 minutes, allowing them to breathe and filter the water, expelling any sand from inside the shells.
- Remove the beards from the mussels (these are little brown threads that may be sticking out from between the two shells.) Grasp the threads and pull them out towards the hinge end of the mussel.
- Remove the mussels from the bowl of water with a slotted spoon and place in a fresh bowl. Rinse the mussels again and pat dry.
- In a large hot pan, add the white wine and mussels and mix vigorously. Add the butter compound and cover the pan with a lid. Continue cooking for 3–4 minutes until mussels have opened. Discard any mussels that don't open.
- To serve, add the mussels to a large bowl. Sprinkle with parsley. Serve with wedges of crusty bread on the side.

Note: Larger amounts of compound butter can be kept for 2 weeks as long as they are covered and remain refrigerated.

IKA MATA

Quite literally the term means raw fish, served traditionally in the Cook Islands. It's worth using a good quality fish for this dish. We use Gurnard or Kingfish at The Cove, but a firm white fish will work perfectly.

Serves 4–6
Preparation time: 30 minutes

INGREDIENTS

500 g (17½ oz) firm white fish,
   (gurnard, hapuka, kingfish), diced
juice of 1–2 lemons
1 teaspoon garlic, crushed
1 teaspoon ginger, crushed
1 Lebanese (telegraph) cucumber,
   diced
1 red pepper, diced
1 yellow pepper, diced
1 tablespoon red onion, diced
zest of 1 lime
½ tablespoon coriander (cilantro)
   leaves, chopped
¼ medium size chilli, finely chopped
425 ml (14 fl oz) coconut cream
   (tinned is fine)
sea salt and freshly ground pepper
micro salad greens, to garnish
slices coconut, to garnish
lemon wedges, to serve

AVOCADO PURÉE

2 ripe avocados
2 tablespoons sour cream
2 teaspoons lemon juice
sea salt and freshly ground black
   pepper

METHOD

- Dice the fish into small squares and place in a bowl. All the pieces should be equal size so the fish marinates evenly. Pour the lemon juice over the fish to cover. Add the garlic and ginger and mix through. Cover the bowl with cling film and refrigerate for 1 hour.
- Finely dice the cucumber, red pepper, yellow pepper and red onion and combine with the lime zest, coriander and chilli.
- Remove the fish from the refrigerator and strain off lemon juice. Add the diced vegetables to the chilled fish and stir through. Add coconut cream and season to taste. Refrigerate until ready to serve.
- To make the avocado purée, mash the avocados and mix with the sour cream and lemon juice. Blend until smooth and season to taste. Allow to chill.
- Serve in a glass layered with avocado puree at the bottom, marinated fish on top with micro salad greens, slices of coconut and lemon wedges on the side.

BEETROOT-CURED SALMON WITH SMOKED YOGHURT AND SPICED SEEDS

Sweet beetroot and spices infuse the salmon adding to its already rich flavour. The yoghurt's light smoky acidity adds another level of flavor that's complimented by the spiced seeds and hint of fennel.

Serves 2 as an entrée
Preparation time: 1 hour (+ 24 hours prior)

CURED SALMON

2 large beetroots, washed and dried
300 g (10½ oz) castor sugar
300 g (10½ oz) table salt
zest of 1 orange
zest of 1 lemon
1 teaspoon black peppercorns
1 salmon fillet, skinless

SMOKED YOGHURT

200 g (8 oz) Greek yoghurt
1½ tablespoon liquid smoke
pinch of salt

SPICED SEEDS

300 ml (10 oz) canola oil
30 g (1 oz) black rice
10 g (½ oz) sunflower seeds
10 g (½ oz) pumpkin seeds
5 g (¼ oz) fennel seeds
salt, to taste

TO SERVE

olive oil, to drizzle
fresh herbs, to garnish

METHOD

- To cure the salmon, grate the whole beetroot (with skin on) on the coarse side of a cheese grater. Combine all the other ingredients together with the grated beetroot until the mixture is moist. Lay half of the curing mix in a tray and place the skinless fillet of salmon on top. Cover the fillet with the remaining curing mix and allow to cure in the refrigerator for up to 24 hours.
- Once cured, wash the fillet under water and pat dry. Cut 5 mm (⅕ in) thick slices and set aside for plating.
- To make the yoghurt, place a porous cloth in a strainer and add the yoghurt. Place the strainer with yoghurt in the refrigerator with a bowl under the strainer to catch any liquid. Let the yoghurt sit for 4 hours to drain excess water. Once the yoghurt has firmed slightly, place it into a bowl and discard the drained water.
- Mix the liquid smoke with the yoghurt and season with salt.
- To spice the seeds, heat the oil until just before it starts to smoke. Carefully put the black rice into the oil and it will puff up almost immediately. Strain the rice out of the oil and place on a paper towel to absorb any excess oil.
- Toast the seeds together in a non-stick frypan over medium heat for 5 minutes or until they become fragrant. Remove from heat.
- Mix the rice with the toasted seeds and season with salt.
- To serve, place the yoghurt in a piping bag and cut a small hole on the bottom corner of the bag.
- To serve, place salmon slices on to each plate and pipe on several small dots of smoked yoghurt. Sprinkle the seed mix over the top and drizzle with a little olive oil and garnish with fresh herbs.

Note: Liquid smoke is an essence or extract which can be found at specialty food stores.

CRAB RÖSTI WITH POACHED EGGS

A wonderful new addition to The Quay breakfast menu, this dish is a slightly different take on eggs benedict with a nod to south American creole flavours. If you can't source crab meat, substitute with hot smoked salmon.

Serves 2
Preparation time: 40 minutes

CRAB RÖSTI

1 tablespoon olive oil
20 g (1 oz) brown onion, diced
20 g (1 oz) green capsicum (bell peppers), diced
20 g (1 oz) celery, diced
100 g (3½ oz) crab meat
20 g (1 oz) spring onion (scallions), chopped
50 g (2 oz) Panko breadcrumb
2 eggs, lightly beaten
1 tablespoon Dijon mustard
1 tablespoon Worcestershire sauce
1 teaspoon Tabasco sauce
1 teaspoon paprika
1 teaspoon cumin powder
salt and pepper to season
canola oil and butter, for frying

POACHED EGGS

4 free range eggs
1½ L (51 fl oz) water
1 tablespoon white vigegar

TO SERVE

Hollandaise Sauce (p. 23), optional
cream cheese, softened (optional)

METHOD

- Add olive oil to a frypan and cook onion, celery and capsicum on a medium to low heat until soft. Add the crab meat.
- Remove from the heat and add all the remaining ingredients to the mix including salt and pepper to season (except the oil and butter). Combine well, season with salt and pepper and refrigerate for 20 minutes.
- Once the mix has chilled, form into small patties roughly around 70 g (3 oz).
- Fry over a medium heat in canola oil and butter until golden brown. Flip the patty and repeat on the other side.
- To poach the eggs, add hot water and white vinegar to a large pot. Bring to the boil and lower temperature to a gentle simmer. Crack eggs one at a time just above the water surface. Cook eggs for 2 minutes until the whites are opaque but the yolk is still wobbly. Remove from the pan using a slotted spoon.
- To serve, place the crab rösti on plates and add a poached egg on top of each. Spoon over with a little hollandaise sauce or cream cheese (if using).

SEAFOOD CHOWDER

There is an abundance of seafood in New Zealand including scallops, prawns (shrimp) and a white fish similar to terakihi or salmon. This dish makes the most of the local produce.

Serves 6
Preparation time: 1 hour

INGREDIENTS
1 onion, diced
1 carrot, diced
1 fennel bulb, sliced
1 tablespoon garlic, minced
250 g (9 oz) butter, melted
250 ml (8 fl oz) white wine
1 L (34 fl oz) cream
xx g (xx oz) assorted seafood of choice
sea salt and freshly ground pepper

BEURRE MANIE
1 teaspoon butter
1 teaspoon flour

METHOD
- Combine onion, carrot and fennel bulb in a food processor and blend until very fine. Transfer to a large saucepan. Add the garlic and mix in well. Add in the melted butter and white wine and cook until the vegetables are soft. Stir in cream and bring to a simmer, being careful not to let it reach boiling point.
- Add seafood according to size and density and don't overcook as this will make it rubbery.
- To thicken the chowder, make a beurre manie. Combine equal parts of flour and butter mixed together to form a rough dough. Crumble a small amount into the chowder and whisk continuously until combined. Continue adding beurre manie if required until the desired consistency is reached. Season to taste with salt and pepper.

SMOKED FISH GALETTE WITH POTATO HASH

We use Blue Wharehou at The Cove. It's a versatile fish with good texture and it's available all year round.

Serves 6
Preparation time: 40 minutes

INGREDIENTS

1½ kg (53 oz) potatoes
500 g (17½ oz) quality smoked fish, bones removed
handful flat leaf parsley, finely chopped
handful dill, finely chopped
handful chives, finely chopped
olive oil, for greasing tray
6 eggs, for poaching
watercress, to serve

MUSTARD HOLLANDAISE

3 egg yolks
1 whole egg
1 tablespoon lemon juice
250 g (9 oz) melted salted butter (hot)
salt and freshly ground pepper
1 teaspoon grain mustard

METHOD

- Preheat the oven to 200°C (400°F).
- Peel and dice the potatoes. Bring a large saucepan of water to the boil and add the potatoes. Cook until soft, then drain. Using a potato masher, dry mash the potatoes. Add the smoked fish, parsley, dill and chives. Mix together.
- Divide the mixture and form into six 200 g (7 oz) patties.
- Place the patties in a single layer on a non-stick tray with a light film of oil and bake in the oven for 20–30 minutes until base is crisp. Turn patties over and bake for another 20–30 minutes.
- To make the mustard hollandaise, blend the egg yolks, whole egg and lemon juice in a food processor. Add hot melted butter at a slow consistent stream for a strong emulsification. Season with salt and pepper to taste. Add grain mustard and combine. Keep in a warm place until required.
- Bring a pan of water to the boil and reduce the heat. Crack in each egg, making sure they don't separate. Poach for 4 minutes before carefully removing with a spoon.
- To serve, place a soft poached egg on each smoked fish galette, drizzle with mustard hollandaise and garnish with watercress.

Note: This recipe can be made with fried eggs if you prefer.

SEARED BIG EYE TUNA WITH CRAB REMOULADE

An ideal entrée or light lunchtime dish that combines the freshness of citrus with creamy crab remoulade. In the summer months we serve this as part of our seasonal tasting plate.

Serves 4
Preparation time: 1 hour

INGREDIENTS

500 g (17½ oz) yellow fin tuna (mid
  loin)
1–2 tablespoons olive oil
1–2 teaspoons Cajun Spice Mix
  (p. 141)

ORANGE AND FENNEL SALAD

3 large oranges
1 fennel bulb, thinly sliced
large handful watercress, washed
Citrus Vinaigrette, (p. 136)

CRAB REMOULADE

4 tablespoons crab meat (or 3–4 diced
  prawns per person)
Tartare Sauce, (p. 141)
½ spring onion (scallion), chopped

METHOD

- Roll the tuna in olive oil and dust with Cajun seasoning. In a hot pan, heat tuna for 15 seconds on each side including the edges. Avoid blackening the coating. Remove from the heat and set aside.
- To prepare the salad and remoulade, segment the oranges and toss together with sliced fennel and washed watercress. Place in a bowl and dress with vinaigrette.
- Mix tartare sauce, spring onion and crab meat together.
- Slice the tuna thinly, pinching the sides as you slice to ensure a nice even cut.
- Serve portions of tuna alongside the crab remoulade. Add orange and fennel salad and sprinkle with freshly ground pepper.

COVE CEASAR SALAD

This light tasty dish is ideal for an easy summer lunch. We've created the recipe with chicken but it also works well with yellow fin tuna.

Serves 4–6
Preparation time: 40 minutes

INGREDIENTS

4 tablespoons olive oil, for baking
3 large chicken breasts
1 cos lettuce, washed
large bunch spinach leaves
6 bacon rashers (pancetta)
6 free range eggs, poached (p. 107)
Anchovy Mayonnaise (p. 140)
Citrus Vinaigrette (p. 136)
Baked Saffron Polenta (p. 75), to serve

METHOD

- Preheat oven to 160°C (325°F).
- Add oil to an ovenproof dish. Add chicken and coat thoroughly with the oil in the dish. Roast in the oven until cooked but tender, about 20–25 minutes.
- Grill the bacon on a medium to high temperature for a couple of minutes under a grill (broiler). Remove and drain.
- Wash cos lettuce and spinach leaves and dress with the citrus vinaigrette.
- Remove the chicken from the oven. Allow to rest for about 5 minutes. Make the baked saffron potenta as per recipe on p. 75 cut into the size of croutons.
- To serve, slice the chicken into chunky portions and place in a serving bowl layering with the chopped bacon and salad greens. Add the poached eggs on top and finish with anchovy mayonnaise. Sprinkle polenta croutons in the salad and serve immediately.

OYSTERS WITH MIGNONETTE SAUCE

Lloyd was captivated by the food and lifestyle that Paris offered. He first tried oysters at one of the many street stalls set up in the city. At The Cove, we serve fresh Clevedon oysters with this simple shallot and vinegar dressing. If you are buying fresh oysters, you may need to shuck them so we have included this process in the recipe.

Serves 4 (entrée size)
Preparation time: 30 minutes

INGREDIENTS

1 dozen oysters
60 ml (2 fl oz) white wine vinegar
90 ml (3 fl oz) red wine vinegar
1 teaspoon freshly ground black
  pepper
2 small French shallots, peeled, very
  finely diced
sea salt

METHOD

- To shuck fresh oysters, using an oyster knife and wearing protective gloves, hold the oyster, cup down, in one hand with the back (or hinge) facing you. Alternatively, hold the oyster on top of a kitchen towel placed on a flat surface. Holding the oyster in one hand, with your other, insert the tip of the knife in the hinge and push down, twisting the knife slightly. This should release the top shell from the bottom shell.
- Slide the knife inside the oyster, and move it along the inside flat part of the top shell. This will cut the oyster's muscle from the top shell.
- Slide the knife under the oyster to release it from the bottom shell.
- Combine the white and red wine vinegar, ground pepper and shallots in a bowl. Season with sea salt. Set aside for 15 minutes to allow the flavours to develop.
- To serve, cover a flat dish with crushed ice. Drizzle the dressing over each oyster and place on the serving dish.

Note: Avoid using a regular knife to shuck oysters. Not only is there a much greater risk of injury, but an oyster knife is stronger than a kitchen knife which can easily break. The gloves are important because it's possible for the knife to slip, or even pierce the shell. Feel free to double the quantity if you love oysters.

SMOKED SALMON AND LENTIL SALAD

We use Matakana hot-smoked salmon and flake it on the top in generous chunks. As a guide, use about 100 g (3½ oz) of chunky flaked hot smoked salmon per person as it is very rich.

Serves 4
Preparation time: 1 hour

INGREDIENTS

1 medium carrot, finely diced
2 celery sticks, finely diced
1 medium onion, finely diced
400 g (14 oz) hot-smoked salmon fillet
2 cloves garlic, crushed
1 teaspoon curry powder
pinch of dried thyme
400 g (14 oz) Puy lentils
2 L (68 fl oz) chicken stock
juice of 1 lemon
1 tablespoon olive oil
4 free range eggs, poached (p. 107)
1 fennel bulb, thinly sliced, to garnish
micro salad greens, to garnish

METHOD

- Dice carrots, celery, and onion into small pieces. Add olive oil to a fry pan on a medium heat then add onions and cook until soft and translucent. Add crushed garlic cloves, curry powder, dried thyme and lentils. Stir and cover with chicken stock, increasing the heat and gradually bringing to the boil. Lower heat and simmer until the lentils are al dente. Strain the lentil mix and while they're still hot, add lemon juice and olive oil to taste.
- Season with salt and pepper and serve at room temperature.
- Serve the lentils with a soft poached egg on top. Flake the hot-smoked salmon over and garnish with thinly sliced fennel and micro greens.

SNAPPER WITH CITRUS RISOTTO AND BEETROOT LENTIL SALAD

We prefer to cook fish with the skin on where possible. It protects the flesh, has great nutrients and is delicious when it's crisped in a frypan.

Serves 6
Preparation time: 2 hours

RISOTTO

1 onion, finely diced
1 teaspoon garlic, crushed
100 g (3½ oz) butter
250 g (9 oz) Arborio rice
salt and pepper to taste
750 ml (25 fl oz) fish stock
150 g (5 oz) Parmesan cheese, shaved
zest of 3 limes
2 teaspoons lemon juice

SALAD

250 g (9 oz) baby beets
250 g (9 oz) puy lentils
150 ml (5 fl oz) Citrus Vinaigrette
   (p. 136)
sprig of fresh tarragon, finely chopped

SNAPPER

6 medium fillets of snapper
2 tablespoons oil (or clarified butter)
pinch flaky sea salt
micro salad greens, to garnish

METHOD

- To make the risotto , fry the onions and garlic in butter ensuring they don't brown. Add the Arborio rice and continue to fry without the onions colouring. Add a pinch of salt and pepper.
- Heat the fish stock in a separate pan and when hot add 250 ml (8 fl oz) to the rice, stirring continuously until the liquid has absorbed. Repeat this step with another 250 ml (8 fl oz) of stock, stirring until all the liquid has been absorbed.
- Add the remaining stock and stir. The rice should be plump, but still al dente. Transfer the contents to a clean dish and add shaved Parmesan and zest of three limes.
- Stir the mixture and set aside to allow to cool. Cover and chill in the refrigerator for a couple of hours.
- Preheat oven to 200°C (400°F).
- Remove risotto from the refrigerator and form into 150 g patties.
- Place on a non-stick oven tray and bake at until crisp and golden.
- To make the salad, boil the baby beets until tender. Remove the skins and cut into cubes (with gloves to stop staining).
- Cook the lentils in plenty of salted water until softened, but still nutty in texture. Discard excess liquid.
- Add the vinaigrette to the lentils while still hot as they will absorb the dressing more easily. Add cubed beetroot and chopped tarragon.
- Score the snapper skin by pinching the fish firmly and moving a sharp knife across it. Be careful not to cut the

flesh too deeply. This prevents the fillet from curling during cooking and will ensure it's cooked more evenly.

- Heat oil in a heavy-based frypan. Season the fish thoroughly with a generous pinch of sea salt and place skin down into a hot frypan. Reduce the heat immediately to avoid the skin from burning. Once the skin is crisp, turn the fish and continue cooking: be careful not to overcook. Allow a couple of minutes each side as the fish will continue cooking even when removed from the pan.
- To serve, place the snapper on top of the risotto patties and add generous spoonfuls of the salad. Garnish with a handful of micro greens.

SEARED SCALLOPS WITH AVOCADO, COCONUT AND MANGO SALAD

South Pacific in style, this dish is perfect for serving outdoors in summer.

Serves 4–6
Preparation time: 1 hour

DRESSING

1 red onion, peeled and finely sliced
125 ml (4 fl oz) red wine vinegar
1 teaspoon mild curry powder
1–2 fresh mangos
30 g (1 oz) coriander (cilantro) leaves
375 ml (12 fl oz) canola oil
flaky sea salt and ground pepper to
   taste

SALAD

1 fresh coconut
1 Lebanese (telegraph) cucumber,
   seeds removed
2 ripe avocados
handful of pea feathers
400 g (14 oz) scallops
pinch flaky sea salt
½–1 tablespoon olive oil

METHOD

- To make the dressing, combine onion slices and red wine vinegar and leave to stand for an hour. This will allow the onion to absorb the colour of the red wine vinegar.
- Toast curry powder in a dry pan to release fragrance and add to the onion.
- Peel and dice mango flesh and combine with the onion. Add in coriander and canola oil. Season with flaky sea salt and ground pepper. Refrigerate overnight if making in advance.
- To prepare the salad, first open the coconut. Tap a large clean nail through the eye holes of the coconut and drain the water into a glass. Tap the coconut firmly with a hammer, rotating between strikes to remove hard shell. Peel long shavings of coconut using a potato peeler.
- Thinly slice cucumber into similar size pieces and peel and slice avocado.
- Arrange salad ingredients on a plate and spoon dressing over the salad.
- Remove scallops from the refrigerator 15 minutes prior to cooking. Pat dry to remove excess moisture and season with flaky sea salt. Lightly coat the scallops with olive oil.
- Heat a frypan to medium-high and sear scallops to achieve a golden caramel colour. Don't overcrowd the pan and resist overcooking. Remove from the pan.
- To serve, place salad on plates, add fish on top and finish with a handful of pea feathers scattered over.

Note: The dressing can be made a day earlier to allow the flavours to fully develop.

PAN-FRIED JOHN DORY WITH ROASTED ASPARAGUS AND BISQUE SAUCE

A beautifully moist dish that appears on the summer menu at The Cove.

Serves 4–6
Preparation time: 2 hours

BISQUE SAUCE

125 ml (4 fl oz) olive oil
½ onion, finely sliced
1 small carrot, finely sliced
1 small fennel bulb, finely sliced
1 teaspoon crushed garlic
2 tablespoon tomato paste
250g (9oz) frozen whole prawns
1 tablespoon chopped thyme
1 L (32 fl oz) chopped peeled
   tomatoes (canned is fine)
sea salt and pepper

PARSNIP PURÉE

3 large parsnips, chopped
250 ml (8 fl oz) cream
sea salt and pepper

FISH AND ASPARAGUS

18 asparagus spears
sea salt and pepper
2 teaspoons olive oil 6 fillets John
   Dory (or snapper)
1 tablespoon olive oil (or clarified
   butter)
sea salt and freshly ground black
   pepper
parsnip strips, thinly sliced and fried,
   to garnish

METHOD

- Preheat oven 180°C (350°F).
- To make the bisque sauce, heat oil to a frypan. Add sliced onion, carrot, fennel and the garlic and cook over a gentle heat until soft.
- Add the tomato paste and blend over a gentle heat for 2 minutes. Add the frozen prawns, thyme, tomatoes and season accordingly. Cook sauce on a low heat until the prawns are completely cooked. Remove the heads from the prawns and blend the sauce through a fine sieve.
- To make the parsnip purée, add parsnips and cream to a saucepan. Cook gently until the parsnip is soft, adding more cream if necessary. Once cooked, place in a food processor and blend until smooth. Season to taste.
- Preheat oven to 180°C (350°F).
- Trim the asparagus spears. Season with salt and pepper and place on a baking tray greased with olive oil. Place in oven and cook for 5 minutes.
- To prepare the fish, score the skin by pinching the fish firmly and moving a sharp knife across to prevent the fillet from curling, being careful not to cut the flesh to deeply. Season with salt and pepper. Heat a frypan with the olive oil on a moderate to high heat. Place the fish skin side down into the pan and cook until a crust forms. Adjust heat if necessary to avoid burning the skin. Turn the fish and continue until the fish is lightly cooked through.
- To serve, spoon the parsnip purée on a plate and add 3 asparagus spears. Place the pan-fried John Dory as a centerpiece, ladle a few tablespoons of bisque sauce over the top with crisp parsnip strips. Sprinkle ground black pepper to finish.

BLACK AND BLUE TUNA WITH MISO MAYONNAISE AND BRAISED KELP

John Salisbury, head chef at The Quay brought this recipe with him from Melbourne and it has become one of the most popular dishes on the summer menu. A dish that makes the most of both raw tuna sashimi and seared tuna, matched with a blend of traditional Japanese seasonings, furikake and miso.

Serves 1–2
Preparation time: 30 minutes

MISO MAYONNAISE
100 g (4 oz) Kewpie mayonnaise
20 g (1 oz) white miso paste
juice of half a lemon

BRAISED KELP
25 g (1 oz) kombu leaves
100 ml (3½ oz) soy sauce
100 ml (3½ oz) mirin
100 ml (3½ oz) water

TUNA
150 g (5 oz) Raw yellowfin tuna (or other variety of sashimi grade)
1 tsp furikake seasoning

METHOD
- Mix the miso paste with the mayonnaise and the lemon juice. Place in a piping bag, cut a small hole in the bottom corner of the bag and set aside.
- To make the braised kelp, mix the liquids together in a saucepan. Add the kombu and cover with a lid to simmer for 10 minutes. Shake the pan to mix the kombu every couple of minutes.
- Remove from the heat and allow to cool in the pot. Once cool enough to handle, remove the kombu from the liquid and set aside for serving.
- Cook the tuna on a very hot chargrill or hotplate on one side only (black) and leave the other side raw (blue).
- To serve, cut the tuna in half and place the two pieces on a plate, one black side up and the other blue side up. Pipe a few dots of miso mayonnaise around the plate and place a few kombu strips across the tuna. Sprinkle furikake seasoning over the plate.

Note: Miso is a traditional Japanese seasoning made from fermented soybeans. Furikake is a dry Japanese seasoning made from dried and ground seaweed, sesame seeds, sugar and salt. These ingredients together with Kewpie mayonnaise are available in the Japanese condiments section of most supermarkets.

GRAVLAX

Lloyd first sampled this dish in Denmark and has loved it ever since. Essentially, gravlax is salmon that's been cured with salt and sugar and infused with the flavour of fresh dill. Order sushi grade salmon to ensure freshness and you can adjust the ratio of sugar to salt depending on your taste. Plan to eat the gravlax within a few days after it's been cured.

Serves 10
Preparation time: 30 minutes plus 2–3 days curing time

INGREDIENTS

55 g (2 oz) sugar
2 tablespoons coarse sea salt
1 teaspoon ground black peppercorns
2½ kg (5½ lb) salmon, filleted, skin on
1 tablespoon vodka (or brandy)
2 tablespoons dill, finely chopped
2 tablespoons dill, chopped (extra)

TO SERVE

mustard sauce (store bought)
pumpernickel bread (or bread/crackers of choice)
shot of vodka, chilled (per person)

METHOD

- Combine sugar, salt and ground peppercorns in a dish.
- Remove any remaining bones from the salmon. Pat dry salmon paper towel and lay fillet skin-side down on a tray.
- Splash the salmon with half the vodka or brandy and rub half the sugar mixture into the salmon fillet. Sprinkle over with dill.
- Repeat the process on the second fillet then lay it flesh side down on top of the first fillet. Seal with plastic wrap and place a heavy chopping board or similar object on top. This helps to press moisture out of the fish as it cures. Refrigerate overnight, turning every 12 hours. Two days will be sufficient to lightly cure the salmon or three days to make it firmer.
- Unwrap the salmon, laying both fillets on a board. Remove the seasoning and dill with a dry pastry brush. Sprinkle the fresh chopped dill and serve whole or thinly sliced.
- Option to serve with a traditional mustard sauce and pumpernickel bread/crackers and a shot of chilled vodka.

DRESSINGS AND SIDES

The only way to make a dish stand out, is to dress it up.

Other than the fact that salad vegetables look lively after being tossed in a dressing, there's also the major benefit of intensifying the flavours. We've selected a few favourite dressings and sides to ignite any fresh leafy salad and to accompany the seafood and meat dishes.

A delicious French vinaigrette is optimal for any summer salad, and a fresh herb pesto or Cajun spice mix is perfect to enhance fish and chicken dishes.

CITRUS VINAIGRETTE

INGREDIENTS

1 tablespoon garlic, crushed
2 lemons, zest and juiced
50 ml (11½ fl oz) red wine vinegar
1½ tablespoons wholegrain mustard
2 tablespoons thyme (or rosemary), chopped
750 ml (24 fl oz) canola oil (or sunflower oil)
salt and pepper, to season

METHOD

- Blend all the ingredients together and season accordingly. Refrigerate in a glass container.

SPICED SOUR CREAM

INGREDIENTS

250 g (9 oz) sour cream
250 g (9 oz) whole egg mayonnaise
60 ml (2 fl oz) milk
40 g (1½ oz) tomatoes, chopped
1 tablespoon garlic, minced
½ onion, finely chopped
1 teaspoon dried parsley
1 teaspoon dried dill
5 ml (¼ fl oz) Tabasco sauce (or favourite chilli sauce)
1 teaspoon cumin
1 teaspoon cayenne pepper
1 teaspoon black pepper
1 teaspoon salt
2 limes, zest and juice

METHOD

- Combine all the ingredients together and blend to make a spicy sauce for pizzas or burgers. Store in a glass jar and refrigerate.

PICKLED RED ONIONS

INGREDIENTS

500 g (17½ oz) red onions, thinly sliced and salted
200 g (7 oz) caster sugar
200 ml (7 fl oz) red wine vinegar

METHOD

- Place the onions in a bowl.
- In a pot, bring the sugar and vinegar to the boil and pour over the onions. Cover and leave to cool.

FETA AND SUNDRIED TOMATO DIP

INGREDIENTS

250 g (9 oz) cow's feta
25 g (1 oz) sundried tomatoes, crushed
1 teaspoon thyme, chopped
1 teaspoon olive oil
freshly ground black pepper

METHOD

- Combine feta, sundried tomatoes and thyme in a bowl. Add a small amount of olive oil and season with black pepper to taste.
- Refrigerate until ready to serve.

ANCHOVY MAYONNAISE

Serves 4
Preparation time: 20 minutes

INGREDIENTS

2 free range eggs, poached (p. 107)
3 anchovy fillets
6 cloves Confit Garlic (p. 140)
25 ml (1 fl oz) red wine vinegar
25 ml (1 fl oz) lemon juice
50 g (2 oz) Parmesan cheese
300 ml (10 fl oz) olive oil (or garlic oil from the confit)
sea salt and freshly ground pepper

METHOD

- Make the poached eggs as per instructions on page xx. Blend warm poached eggs with anchovy fillets and 6 garlic cloves.
- Add red wine vinegar, lemon juice and Parmesan to combine. Slowly add the oil and keep mixing until you have a creamy emulsion.
- Season to taste after checking the saltiness of anchovies and adjust accordingly.
- Keep in the refrigerator.

Note: You'll have enough to use as a topping for four serves. Keep any left over mayonnaise for up to one month in the refrigerator.

GARLIC CONFIT

INGREDIENTS

25 garlic cloves, peeled
250 ml (18 fl oz) olive oil

METHOD

- Place the garlic and oil in a saucepan over a very low heat, being careful not to boil. Gently poach for 1 hour until the garlic is soft.
- Transfer the garlic and oil to a sterilised glass jar, seal and store in the refrigerator for up to 3 months.

TARTARE SAUCE

INGREDIENTS
75 g (3 oz) gherkins
40 g (1½ oz) capers
40 g (1½ oz) white onion
750 ml (25 fl oz) Garlic Aioli (p. 142)

1 lemon, zest and juice

METHOD
· Finely chop the gherkins, capers and white onion and combine with the aioli, lemon juice and zest.
· Refrigerate in a glass jar.

CAJUN SPICE MIX

INGREDIENTS
8 tablespoons paprika
2½ tablespoons salt
2½ tablespoons garlic powder
2½ tablespoons onion powder
2 tablespoons cayenne pepper
2 tablespoons white pepper
2 tablespoons black pepper
4 teaspoons dried thyme
4 teaspoons dried basil
4 teaspoons oregano
2 teaspoons cumin
2 teaspoons allspice

METHOD
· Combine ingredients together to make spice mix. This can be stored and used as a Cajun seasoning for chicken or fish.
· Store in a glass jar to stay fresh.

GARLIC AIOLI

Aioli originates from the Mediterranean and is made using garlic and olive oil and may also include egg. It's a superb accompaniment to crispy potatoes, chargrilled vegetables and fish.

INGREDIENTS

6 egg yolks
175 g (6 oz) Garlic Confit (p. 140)
125 ml (4 fl oz) red wine vinegar
1½ L (51 fl oz) confit garlic oil
60 g (2 oz) wholegrain mustard
sea salt and freshly ground pepper, to taste

METHOD

- Place the yolks in a food processor and add confit garlic (making sure it has cooled completely) and blend until smooth.
- Add half the red wine vinegar to the mixture and blend.
- Pour the oil into the food processor at a steady stream. If you find the mix doesn't incorporate, use the remaining red wine vinegar to thin out, and continue adding the remaining oil until it has combined smoothly.
- Add the mustard and seasoning and mix together.

Note: The aioli should have a similar consistency to mayonnaise.

OLIVE TAPENADE

INGREDIENTS

200 g (7 oz) Kalamata olives, finely chopped
250 ml (8 fl oz) Basil Pesto (p. 143)
1 anchovy fillet, chopped

METHOD

- Combine the olives, basil pesto and anchovy fillets to make the tapenade. This can be done using a processor or by hand using a mortar and pestle.
- Refrigerate in a glass jar.

BASIL PESTO

INGREDIENTS

2 bunches fresh basil
1 teaspoon garlic, crushed
2 tablespoons toasted pine nuts
100 g (3 ½ oz) Parmesan cheese, grated
250 ml (8 fl oz) olive oil
salt and pepper, to taste

METHOD

- Combine all ingredients together and blend. Add salt and pepper to taste.
- Store in the refrigerator in a glass container.

CORIANDER PESTO

INGREDIENTS

50 g (2 oz) coriander (cilantro) leaves, fresh
1 tablespoon cashew nuts, toasted
1 clove garlic
20 g (1 oz) Parmesan cheese
100 ml (3 fl oz) olive oil

METHOD

- Blend all the ingredients together and season to taste.

BEST "GOOD MORNING" YOU CAN GET!

SWEET THINGS

Life is uncertain. Eat dessert first.
Ernestine Ulmer

Desserts are always a last option on a restaurant menu and only materialise on the table if diners have sufficient appetite for them. Most of the sweet options at The Quay to The Cove are the result of a creative collaboration between head chefs, Craig and John. A few of them have been on the menu since The Cove first opened and have become firm favourites.

With the success of The Cove and the warm reception from locals, Lloyd managed to segue easily from rural countryside to coastal life in Northland. Not one to sit on his hands for long, and always receptive to new ideas, another unique opportunity presented itself in the form of a waterfront property at 31 Quayside in Whangarei. It was the perfect location in the Town Basin Marina but the existing restaurant was in dire need of a makeover.

'I decided to visit the restaurant known at the time as Reva's, and drank a glass of rosé on the veranda savouring the spectacular marina views. It made quite an impression on me and I kept wondering how I could successfully secure the location.'

Lloyd's initial request for information was met with a series of dead ends. The restaurant owners had previously had forty years in the hospitality business with three separate locations in Whangarei, and Reva's had been a fixture since 1995.

'I had largely given up on the idea when once again fate played a major role in my life.'

A month after he made the visit to Whangarei, a friend told him that the restaurant lease was up for renewal and would soon be offered for tender.

'We set about presenting a case to council that, in my view, couldn't be beaten.'

The concerted effort paid off and Lloyd learnt he'd become the new proprietor of 31 Quayside, which he renamed The Quay. Work on the new restaurant project began almost immediately under the skilful guidance of Waipu builder and friend, Darrel Tucker. The interior was completely redesigned to create an exposed kitchen, a new cocktail bar fabricated from brass and buttoned oyster leather, feature wallpapers sourced from Paris, and Tom Dixon pendant lights to create a sense of decadent luxury. The outdoor dining area overlooks the many yachts berthed in the marina.

Head chef, John Salisbury, was lured from Melbourne and engaged to add artistic flair to the menu. Six months later after much anticipation, The Quay opened.

We finally managed to toast the new restaurant and discuss yet another culinary project in the pipeline, located in the Northland coastal town of Mangawhai. The Dune is a rustic venture that will offer diners the opportunity to enjoy shared tasting plates, sample smoked meats from Highgate Hill, enjoy gourmet pizzas from the wood-fired pizza oven and experience the classic Kiwi barbeque. I asked Lloyd how he managed to sleep at night given the responsibility that comes with running three restaurants. He candidly replied with some simple advice for anyone contemplating a career in hospitality.

'It can be very rewarding, but they better not be afraid of hard work.'

Lloyd's success stems from his dedication and industriousness; but his creative flair and love of food and people, ultimately make his restaurants and recipes something special.

'It's simple really, says Lloyd. 'If you want to succeed, you just have to put your heart into everything you do.'

WHITE CHOCOLATE PANNA COTTA

Traditionally an Italian dessert, this one has a white chocolate twist. The flavours can be varied by using rum or coffee as an alternative to Cointreau, which gives the dish a distinct orange flavour.

Serves 4–6
Preparation time: 40 minutes

PANNA COTTA
500 ml (16 fl oz) cream
50 g (2 oz) caster sugar
50 ml (1½ fl oz) Cointreau
100 g (3½ oz) white chocolate
1½ sheets of gelatin, softened in cold
    water

JELLY
500 g (17 oz) frozen raspberries
100 ml (3½ fl oz) water
100 g (3½ oz) caster sugar
1½ sheets of gelatin, softened in cold
    water
6 mint leaves, to garnish
4–6 scoops gelato, store bought,
    (optional)

METHOD
- Place the cream and caster sugar in a pan to heat. Add the Cointreau, white chocolate and softened gelatin (If using gelatin powder, dissolve 4 teaspoons in 125 ml/4 fl oz hot water then add). Stir occasionally until combined. Remove from the heat and strain through a very fine sieve. Pour into individual dessert glasses and allow to set, about 3–4 hours.
- To make the jelly, place the frozen raspberries, water and caster sugar in a pot and heat. Bring to a simmer and cook for 5 minutes. Add the gelatin stirring occasionally. (If using gelatin powder, dissolve 4 teaspoons in 125 ml/4 fl oz hot water then add this to the pot and stir).
- Pour the liquid through a very fine sieve separating the fruit from the liquid and discard the pulp. Allow the liquid to cool but not set.
- Remove the panna cotta from the refrigerator when set. Carefully pour a layer of jelly over the top.
- Refrigerate for an hour or until jelly has fully set.
- To serve, layer the jelly on top of the panna cotta and garnish with a mint leaf. Add a spoonful of gelato to each serving if you wish.

KEY LIME PIE

Michael's key lime pie is legendary at The Cove. Other than being visually stunning, it has a unique taste sensation that combines a lime zing with a crisp sweet meringue top.

This is a great recipe for a dinner party as the base and meringue can be made a couple of days in advance leaving you more time to entertain your guests on the day/night. A brûlée torch and a sugar thermometer are required for this recipe.

Serves 6–8
Preparation time: 1 hour 30 minutes

BASE
85 g (3 oz) long thread coconut
85 g (3 oz) rolled oats
128 g (4½ oz) malt biscuit crumbs
1 teaspoon vanilla essence
220 g (7¾ oz) brown sugar
200 g (7 oz) softened butter

TOPPING
4 egg yolks
1 tablespoon sugar
400 g (14 oz) condensed milk
200 ml (7 fl oz) cream
6 limes, zest and juice
2 gelatin sheets, softened in cold water
few drops green food colouring

ITALIAN MERINGUE
200 g (7 oz) sugar
200 ml (7 fl oz) water, room temperature
4 egg whites
½ teaspoon white vinegar

METHOD
- Heat oven to 180°C (350°F).
- Put the long thread coconut on an oven tray and bake in the oven at until light golden brown. Repeat this process with the oats on the same temperature until they are a light golden colour. Combine the toasted coconut and oats in a food processor and pulse until fine.
- In a bowl cream the brown sugar and softened butter. Add malt biscuit crumbs and vanilla essence.
- Combine all the base ingredients until they are evenly mixed together to form a large ball. Press the mixture into the base of a greased cake tin or large flan dish and place in the refrigerator to set. This base can be made up to 3 or 4 days in advance and refrigerated.
- To make the topping, separate the 4 egg yolks from the whites, keeping the whites for the Italian Meringue. Place egg yolks and sugar in a metal bowl and whisk constantly over a pot of boiling water till the mix has thickened and turned pale. Take off the heat and add condensed milk, cream, and the lime zest and juice.
- Prepare the gelatin and add to the mix with a few drops of green food colouring. (If using gelatin powder, dissolve 4 teaspoons in 125 ml/4 fl oz hot water). Combine until the green is evenly distributed. Pour the custard mix onto the prepared base and refrigerate until set, allow 1–2 hours.

- To make the meringue, place the sugar and water in a small saucepan and bring to the boil. Use a pastry brush and additional water to brush inside edges of the saucepan regularly, to avoid burning any splattered sugar. Using a sugar thermometer, bring the sugar to 118°C (245°F). When the sugar has reached roughly 105°C (221°F), beat the egg whites and vinegar together so they form soft peaks. Slowly pour the sugar syrup into the egg white mixture and continue beating until the meringue reaches stiff peaks and the bowl is no longer warm.
- Once the meringue is cool, place in a piping bag and refrigerate. This can be made a day in advance.
- To serve, remove the pie from the tin and pipe large peaks of meringue on top until completely covered. Toast with a brûlée torch until the colour changes to a light golden brown. Serve immediately.

Note: For the topping, only combine the sugar with the egg yolks when you are ready to whisk, otherwise the yolks will harden.

CHOCOLATE FONDANT TART

A super dark and delicious dessert offset nicely by the zesty flavours in the berry coulis. All the components of this recipe can be made in advance.

Serves 6
Preparation time: 1½–2 hours

BERRY COULIS
500 g (17½ oz) raspberries (or strawberries)
200 g (7 oz) caster sugar
50 ml (1½ fl oz) water

Tart Pastry (p. 158)
250 g (9 oz) good quality dark chocolate
250 g (9 oz) butter
125 g (4½ oz) caster sugar
5 free range eggs, lightly beaten
5 free range egg yolks
60 g (2½ oz) self-raising (self rising) flour
vanilla ice-cream, store bought, to serve

METHOD
- To make the berry coulis, place berries in a saucepan of water. Add sugar and simmer over a medium heat until the berries break down and the sugar dissolves completely to become a syrup. Pass the syrup through a fine strainer and retain the sauce for serving with the tart. Discard the pulp. This can be made in advance and stored in the refrigerator.
- Preheat oven to 175°C (325°F).
- Make the pastry according to instructions on p. 158 then divide the pastry into 6 individual tart cases. Blind bake by placing a sheet of baking paper on the base and put baking weights, uncooked rice or beans on top of the baking paper. Bake in the oven until the pastry is light golden brown colour, about 10 minutes or until the pastry is firm. These can be made several days in advance and kept in an airtight container until ready to use.
- To make the fondant mixture, add chocolate, butter and sugar in a bowl over a warm pot of water until the chocolate and butter have melted and the sugar dissolved. Set aside to cool.
- Sift self-raising flour into a bowl. Add the eggs and egg yolks and combine. Place the mixture in the refrigerator for at least an hour, preferably overnight.
- Remove the fondant mixture from the refrigerator.
- Preheat the oven to 180°C (350°F).
- Fill the pre-cooked tart shells to just below the brim with the raw fondant mix. Place on a baking tray lined with baking paper and cook in the oven for 8–12 minutes. The fondant should be firm around the edge but still soft in the middle.
- Serve the tarts with berry coulis and vanilla ice-cream on the side.

Note: If you have chocolate fondant mixture left over, this will keep in the refrigerator for up to two weeks.

STICKY DATE PUDDING

One of the most popular winter desserts at The Cove. There's no getting past the fact it's very rich and very filling. It can also be prepared in smaller individual size portions by baking in a 6- or 12-cup ramekin or muffin tray. .

Serves 6–8
Preparation time: 1½ hours

INGREDIENTS

250 g (9 oz) dates, pitted and
   chopped
2 large pears, chopped
250 ml (8 fl oz) water
1¼ teaspoon baking soda
125 g (4½ oz) salted butter, cubed
250 g (9 oz) caster sugar
3 eggs
250 g (9 oz) plain (all purpose) flour,
   sifted
½ tablespoon baking powder, sifted
vanilla bean ice-cream (store bought),
   to serve

BUTTERSCOTCH SAUCE

150 g (5 oz) soft brown sugar
125 g (4½ oz) salted butter
250 ml (8 fl oz) golden syrup
500 ml (16 fl oz) cream

METHOD

- Preheat the oven to 150°C (300°F).
- Combine the dates, pears and water into a saucepan and heat on a low heat until the fruit is soft and the water has evaporated, about 10–15 minutes. Be careful not to over boil the fruit. Add more water if fruit is still not soft and continue to cook until the extra water has evaporated. Mix in the baking soda and set aside.
- In a separate bowl, add the butter and caster sugar. Cream together then add one egg at a time, mixing well each time until blended well.
- Fold in the pear and date fruit mix. Sift in the flour and baking powder and mix to combine.
- Pour the mixture into a lightly greased cake mold and bake at for 1 hour or until cooked. To test, insert a skewer into the middle of the pudding. If it comes out clean, it is ready. If crumbs stick to the sides, put back in oven to cook for a few more minutes and test again.
- To make the butterscotch sauce, combine brown sugar, butter and golden syrup in a pot and bring to a gentle boil. Once the mix has come to the boil, lower the heat and add the cream. Stir the sauce until it starts to thicken and reaches the desired consistency.
- To serve, cut the pudding into dessert-size portions and top with a generous spoonful of butterscotch sauce. Serve with vanilla bean ice-cream.

CRÈME BRÛLÉE

Brûlée is simply the custard or burnt cream that sets the fruit or curd.
We serve a lemon curd crème brûlée or a spiced fruit crème brûlée depending on the season.

Serves 4–6
Preparation time: 1½ hours

INGREDIENTS
9 egg yolks
55 g (2 oz) caster sugar
600 ml (20 fl oz) cream (select a cream with a low butter content)
4 tablespoons Spiced Apple Mix (p. 162), or 4 tablespoons Lemon Curd (p. 159)
150 g (5 oz) raisins
60 ml (2 fl oz) rum
1 teaspoon butter, for greasing

METHOD
- Pre heat oven on 120°C (248°F).
- Beat the egg yolks and sugar together until smooth. Allow to cool to room temperature. Add the cream to the mixture stirring continuously.
- Pass the custard mixture through a very fine sieve and set aside.
- For the spiced fruit mix (if using), follow the recipe for spiced apple mix on p. 162. Soak the raisings in rum for 30 minutes then add to the apple mix for extra spice.
- Place a tablespoon of the spiced fruit mix or lemon curd into lightly greased ramekin dishes (lined with baking paper if you wish) and fill with the custard. Wave a brûlée torch over the surface, at about 5 cm (2 in), to remove bubbles and to give a better finish.
- Pour water into a flat baking tray and place the ramekin dishes in carefully so that the water level reaches about halfway up the sides. Place the baking tray in an oven and bake for 1 hour.
- Remove the brûlée from the oven (it should have just a very slight wobble). Remove from the water bath and allow to cool. Refrigerate for 30 minutes.
- Before you are ready to serve, remove the brûlée from the refrigerator and allow to come to room temperature.
- Sprinkle a layer of caster sugar evenly over each brûlée. Move the brûlée torch very steadily over the sugar until the sugar has caramelized and the top is golden brown and crisp to the touch.
- Serve at room temperature as is – it does need anything else.

Note: You will need a brûlée torch for this recipe.

TARTE AU CITRON

This lovely light lemon tart is perfect with fresh raspberries in season.

Serves 6
Preparation time: 2 hours

TART PASTRY
250 g (9 oz) butter
100 g (3½ oz) sugar
400 g (14 oz) plain (all purpose) flour
2 free range eggs, lightly beaten

FILLING
8 free range eggs
375 g (13 oz) caster sugar
250 ml (8 fl oz) lemon juice
zest of 3 lemons
250 ml (8 fl oz) cream

TO SERVE
fresh seasonal fruit

METHOD
- To make the pastry, cream butter and sugar together in a bowl. Sift in the flour. Add the eggs gradually and work the mix a smooth ball. Cover and place in the refrigerator for 1 hour. If not required immediately, the pastry can be kept in the refrigerator for up to a week.
- To prepare the filling, combine eggs, caster sugar, lemon juice, zest and cream in a bowl and whisk for around 4 minutes.
- Preheat oven to 175°C (325°F).
- Roll the pastry out to fit your tart dish ensuring a smooth thin crust. Blind bake the tart shell by placing a sheet of baking paper on the base and put baking weights, uncooked rice or beans on top of the baking paper. Bake the pastry until the base is a light golden brown, about 20–25 minutes. Remove the paper and weights and return pastry to the oven for another 10 minutes to brown.
- Remove from the oven and cool slightly.
- Reduce oven temperature to 130°C (250°F).
- Pour filling mixture into baked pastry case. Bake until the filling is just set, about 50 minutes.
- Allow to cool at room temperature then refrigerate.
- Before you are ready to serve, remove from the refrigerator and allow to come to room temperature, about 15 minutes.
- Dust tarts with icing sugar and serve with fresh seasonal berries.

LEMON CURD

This piquant lemony blend makes an ideal filling for tarts, cakes and desserts and is equally delicious served on warm, buttered ciabatta.

Makes 1 litre
Preparation time: 30 minutes

INGREDIENTS
500 ml (16 fl oz) lemon juice
500 g (17½ oz) butter
500 g (17½ oz) caster sugar5 free range eggs
10 free range egg yolks

METHOD
· Combine all the ingredients in a bowl and mix together. Place the bowl over a saucepan of simmering hot water making sure no water goes into the bowl.
· Stir occasionally until the mixture is thick and glossy.
· Remove the bowl from the heat and continue to stir the mixture until cooled. Once completely cooled, refrigerate in an airtight glass jar.

Note: This can be refrigerated for several weeks when kept in a glass jar.

SALTED CARAMEL SLICE

A slice of pure sweetness, this is a popular choice for locals wanting a sugar hit to accompany an espresso at The Cove.

Makes 24 slices
Preparation time: 2 hours

BASE
200 g (7 oz) butter
200 g (7 oz) brown sugar
75 g (2½ oz) long thread coconut
75 g (3 oz) rolled oats
200 g (7 oz) self raising (self rising) flour, sifted
3 tablespoons cocoa, sifted

CARAMEL
100 g (3½ oz) butter
80 ml (2½ fl oz) golden syrup
600 g (190 oz) condensed milk
1 tablespoon salt

CHOCOLATE TOPPING
200 g (7 oz) dark chocolate
100 g (3½ oz) white chocolate
90 ml (3 fl oz) canola oil

METHOD
· Preheat the oven to 180°C (350°F). Line a 20 x 30 cm (8 x 11 in) slice tin with baking paper.
· To make the base, cream the butter and brown sugar and slowly add coconut, oats, sifted flour and cocoa to form a moist, cookie dough mixture.
· Press the mixture firmly into the baking tin and place in the oven to bake for 15 minutes.
· For the caramel, combine butter, golden syrup and condensed milk in a medium-sized pot on a low heat and cook until hot. Add the salt and remove from the heat.
· Remove the base from the oven and pour the caramel on top. Return the slice to the oven to cook for a further 30 minutes or until caramel starts to bubble and turn a deep golden colour. Remove from the oven and allow to cool.
· To make the chocolate topping, place the dark chocolate in a saucepan. Add 60 ml (2 fl oz) of the oil and cook until chocolate and oil have combined into a smooth consistency. Pour over the cooling slice.
· Place the white chocolate in a saucepan. Add 30 ml (1 fl oz) of canola oil cook until chocolate and oil have combined into a smooth consistency.
· Gently pour the melted white chocolate in a zig zag pattern over the dark chocolate. Then using a skewer, zig zag in a pattern from one corner to the opposite corner. Turn the tray 90 degrees and repeat the zig zag process once more to create a marbled effect. Allow to set at room temperature (or in the refrigerator) for at least 1 hour.
· Slice to desired size and serve.

Note: This slice can be frozen.

APPLE MAPLE CRUMBLE

We use Granny Smith apples for this crumble as they have a nice tang to counter the sweetness of the maple syrup.

Serves 6
Preparation time: 1½ hours

SPICED APPLE MIX

250 ml (8 fl oz) maple syrup
250 ml (8 fl oz) apple syrup
2 cinnamon sticks
3 star anise
4 Granny Smith apples peeled, core removed and thinly sliced

CAKE MIXTURE

125 g (4½ oz) butter, softened
170 g (5½ oz) caster sugar
2 eggs
250 g (9 oz) self raising (self rising) flour
125 ml (4 fl oz) spiced apple syrup, from Spiced Apple Mix (p. 162)

CRUMBLE TOPPING

125 g (4½ oz) plain (all purpose) flour
60 ml (2 fl oz) maple or apple syrup
85 g (3 oz) caster sugar
50 g (2 oz) butter
40 g (1½ oz) desiccated coconut

TO SERVE

freshly whipped cream, optional
walnut and maple ice-cream (or icecream of choice), optional

METHOD

· Preheat the oven to 140°C (284°F). Grease a 22 cm (9 in) cake tin.
· Heat the syrup and spices in a saucepan until simmering and then add the sliced apples. Cook over a low heat until the apples are soft, but not mushy. Strain the syrup into a container and retain for later. Discard the spices and keep the cooked apple to one side.
· To make the cake mixture, cream the softened and the caster sugar together. Add eggs to the mixture one at a time beating to combine.
· Add the cooled spiced apple syrup and stir. Sift in the self-raising flour and fold through the mixture until combined.
· Pour the cake mixture into the cake tin and layer the cooked apples evenly on top.
· For the crumble, mix all the crumble ingredients in a separate bowl making sure an even crumb is achieved. It should not be too fine, but also not too sticky. Add more flour or syrup as required.
· Crumble the topping over the apples and bake in the oven for an hour or until a skewer comes out clean.
· Serve hot with freshly whipped cream or walnut and maple ice-cream.

PEANUT BUTTER, CHOCOLATE AND BANANA MUFFINS

This is a muffin that kids love. This recipe can be adapted to replace the banana with apple sauce.

Makes 8
Preparation time: 30 minutes

INGREDIENTS

Olive oil spray, for greasing

75 g (3 oz) very ripe banana (or apple sauce)

50 g (2 oz) smooth peanut butter

2 tablespoons agave nectar (or honey)

1 teaspoon vanilla extract

2 tablespoons brown sugar, lightly packed

1 large egg

¼ teaspoon salt

½ teaspoon baking soda

¼ teaspoon baking powder

9 tablespoons gluten free oat flour

60 g (2½ oz) old fashioned gluten free oats

60 g (2½ oz) dark chocolate chips

METHOD

- Preheat the oven to 180°C (350°F). Lightly coat an 8-cup muffin tin with olive oil spray. If you have a muffin tray with more than 8 cups, half fill the others with water to ensure the heat is distributed evenly.
- Mash the banana in a large bowl. Add peanut butter (do not warm up), agave nectar/honey, vanilla extract and brown sugar. Mix until completely combined, then add egg, salt, baking soda, baking powder and oat flour.
- To make the oat flour, take the old-fashioned oats and pulse them in a blender or food processor until they are a flour-like consistency. Stir in the oats and the dark chocolate chips. Using a deep spoon, place two scoops of the dough into each muffin cavity.
- Bake for 15–18 minutes.

Note: Please avoid using muffin liners for this recipe. Slightly under-baking these muffins will keep them moist and light. If you prefer a sweeter muffin, increase the brown sugar by 1–2 tablespoons.

GLUTEN FREE LEMON AND LIME FRIANDS

French in origin, the friand is a petite cake lighter in texture to a muffin. We make ours gluten-free, but you can also use almond flour as an option.

Makes 8
Preparation time: 40 minutes

INGREDIENTS

olive oil spray
375 g (13 oz) icing sugar
312 g (11 oz) ground almonds
150 g (5 oz) desiccated coconut
2 teaspoons baking powder
200 g (14 oz) butter
8 free range egg whites
4 limes, zest and juice
4 lemons, zest and juice
8 tablespoons unsweetened yoghurt
  (optional), to serve

METHOD

- Preheat the oven to 170°C (325°F) on a fan bake setting. Spray each friand/muffin cup with olive oil spray and line with baking paper if you wish.
- Combine together icing sugar, almonds, coconut and baking powder in a bowl.
- Melt the butter. Zest and juice the lemons and limes and place in a separate bowl.
- Whisk the egg whites until soft peaks form.
- Add the zest and juice to the dry ingredients. Stir in the melted butter. Add the egg whites and gently fold until completely combined.
- Spoon mix into each muffin cup until it is ¾ full. Do not overfill or they will collapse.
- Bake in the oven for 20 minutes or until cooked. Test by inserting a skewer into one. If it comes out clean, the friands are ready. Remove from oven and allow to cool. Then turn out friands from the tray.
- Serve with dollops of unsweetened yogurt if you wish.

STRAWBERRY, BALSAMIC AND LEMON CURD MUFFINS

Who says muffins are boring? We've spiced things up at The Cove combining sweet berries and adding savoury balsamic flavours to the mix.

Makes 14
Preparation time: 30 minutes

INGREDIENTS

olive oil or similar spray, for greasing
250 g (9 oz) caster sugar
620 g (22 oz) self-raising (self rising) flour
400 g (14 oz) frozen strawberries
400 g (14 oz) butter, softened
500 ml (16 fl oz) milk
4 free range eggs
125 ml (4 fl oz) balsamic vinegar
200 g (7 oz) Lemon Curd (p. 159)

METHOD

- Preheat oven to 180°C (350°F) and spray the individual muffin tray cups with olive oil spray.
- Add the sugar to a bowl and sift in the self-raising flour.
- Defrost the frozen strawberries, breaking up with a fork until they're soft and in small chunks.
- Melt the butter and whisk together with milk and eggs. Combine with the strawberries and balsamic vinegar, being careful not to over mix. Spoon muffin dough into muffin cups up to three quarters full.
- Put the lemon curd into a piping bag and insert the nozzle into the muffin (roughly halfway). Inject the equivalent of one tablespoon of curd into each.
- Place the tray in the oven and bake for 20 minutes or until a skewer comes out clean.

CARROT AND BANANA CAKE

This is an easy recipe and as we often have families with young children dining at The Cove, we like to offer something sweet that's still healthy.

Serves 6
Preparation time: 1½ hours

INGREDIENTS

olive oil spray, for greasing
100 g (3½ oz) brown sugar
3 eggs
250 ml (8 fl oz) sunflower (or vegetable oil)
200 g (7 oz) banana, mashed
120 g (4 oz) carrot, grated
80 g (3 oz) walnuts, chopped
160 g (5½ oz) plain (all purpose) flour
60 g (2 oz) self raising (self rising) flour
1 teaspoon baking soda
1 teaspoon mixed spice
½ teaspoon cinnamon
Cream Cheese Icing
50 g (2 oz) butter, softened
125 g (4½ oz)cream cheese
375 g (12 oz) icing sugar

TO SERVE

handful of dried apricots, chopped (optional)
handful of walnuts, roughly chopped (optional)

METHOD

- Preheat oven to 140°C (350°F) and spray a 22 cm (8½ in) cake tin with olive oil spray.
- Cream together the sugar and eggs until the mix forms a pale color. Add oil, banana, carrot, and walnuts to the egg mixture and combine.
- Sift the flours, baking soda, mixed spice and cinnamon into the mixture until evenly combined. Pour the cake batter into the cake tin and bake for 1 hour, or until a skewer comes out clean.
- To make the icing, combine butter and cream cheese in a food processor and slowly add icing sugar. The consistency should be smooth and spreadable.
- Once the cake is cool turn out from the tin and cover with icing.
- To serve, cut into portions and sprinkle each with dried apricots or walnuts if you wish.

APRICOT AND BERRY SHORTCAKE

An ideal winter cake that the whole family will appreciate. Apricots can be substituted with other dried fruits if preferred.

Serves 6
Preparation time: 1 hour

INGREDIENTS
120 g (4 oz) butter,softened
250 g (9 oz) sugar
1 free range egg
125 g (4½ oz) plain (all purpose) flour
2 teaspoons baking powder
150 g (5 oz) dried apricots
250 g (9 oz) mixed frozen berries

TO SERVE
freshly whipped cream (optional)
vanilla bean ice-cream, store bought
   (optional)

METHOD
- Preheat the oven to 180°C (350°F) and line a 25 cm (9 in) tin with baking paper. Defrost the berries and drain off the juice.
- Soak the apricots in hot water for around 20 minutes or until soft and rehydrated. Drain off the water and retain the apricots.
- In a deep bowl, cream the softened butter with the sugar and beat in the egg. Sift the flour and the baking powder and combine into the mixture. Press ⅔ of the cake mix into the lined tin to form a base.
- Chop the softened apricots and mix with the berries. Pour the apricot and berry mix over the cake base and then layer the remaining cake mix in spoonful size dollops on top. This doesn't look so appealing raw, but as the cake rises, the dollops join together leaving small pockets of apricot/ berry mix peeping through.
- Bake for 30–40 minutes. To test if ready, the cake should bounce back when touched lightly. Remove and allow to cool.
- Slice into rectangles and serve with freshly whipped cream or vanilla bean ice-cream if you wish.

PISTACHIO CHAI MUFFINS

A cake with tea all in one. This is a novel way to explore chai tea, blended with the flavours of roasted pistachios.

Makes 8
Preparation time: 30 minutes

INGREDIENTS

250 ml (8 fl oz) milk
1 tablespoon lemon juice
150 g (5 oz) plain (all purpose) flour
85 g (3 oz) wholewheat plain (all purpose) flour
175 g (6 oz) brown sugar
1 teaspoon baking powder
1 teaspoon baking soda
¼ teaspoon salt
30 g (1½ oz) pistachios, roasted, unsalted and finely chopped
60 ml (12 fl oz) canola oil
1 teaspoon pure vanilla extract
1 large egg
4 teaspoons chai tea

METHOD

- Preheat oven to 170°C (325°F) and line muffin tray cups with paper liners (or use olive oil spray).
- Pour the milk into a medium bowl and drizzle in the lemon juice, letting the milk and lemon juice sit for 3 minutes without stirring.
- Sift the flours, baking powder, baking soda and salt into a separate bowl. Add the sugar and pistachios and blend together.
- To the bowl with the milk and lemon juice, add the oil, vanilla and egg and stir.
- Add the wet ingredients to the dry ingredients, being careful not to over mix. Spoon two tablespoons of the muffin dough into the muffin cups (¾ full) and bake for about 20 minutes or until a skewer comes out clean.
- Cool completely before removing the muffins from the trays.
- Serve immediately or keep in an airtight container for a couple of days.

Note: Chai tea is readily available in most supermarkets and food stores.

ORANGE AND ALMOND CAKE WITH LEMON CURD MASCARPONE

A lovely gluten free cake that combines sweet fragrant citrus with the subtlety of mascapone.

Makes 10–12 slices
Preparation time: 40 minutes

CAKE

2 medium size oranges (rind left on)
310 g (11 oz) castor sugar
2 eggs
310 g (11 oz) ground almonds
2 teaspoons baking powder
icing sugar, for dusting

LEMON CURD MASCARPONE

250 g mascarpone
250 g Lemon Curd (p. 159)

METHOD

- Preheat oven to 170°c (325°F) and lightly grease two 20 cm (8 in) cake tins.
- Place oranges in a pot and fill with water to just cover. Bring the water to boil then drain. Repeat the process two more times to remove the strong pith taste. After the third boil, put the cooked whole oranges into a food processor and blend.
- Add sugar and eggs one by one to the food processor and blend to combine. Add ground almond and baking powder. (It's preferable to have texture with this cake so avoid overly blending the mixture.)
- Pour the mix into the two cake tins and bake for 25 minutes.
- Leave to cool in the trays and then turn out upside down onto a cooling rack.
- To make the lemon curd mascarpone, combine the mascarpone with the lemon curd. Spread the mascarpone mix on the base of one of the cakes and carefully position the other cake on top. Refrigerate for at least 1 hour before serving.
- Slice into rectangular portions and dust over with icing sugar.

Note: Avoid overprocessing, keep the mixture as textured as possible to get the full flavours.

CHEESEBOARD

Although not a sweet thing, many people prefer a cheeseboard after a main meal or sometimes after dessert. We are including a cheeseboard in the Sweet Things for this reason and because New Zealand produces some wonderful cheeses worthy of mention.

Lloyd's insatiable appetite for vintage cheeses was cultivated after many weekend trips to Amsterdam.

The French traditionally enjoy a cheeseboard at the end of the meal, the English prefer it between entrée and main course, but at The Cove we enjoy good cheese at any time of the day.

Flavour and textural contrasts are key when it comes to serving a cheeseboard. Select various cheeses based on their creaminess, tangy tones, earthy notes or simply for their mildness.

It's best not to overwhelm the cheeseboard. Between three and five different cheeses is sufficient with a couple of bread and cracker options.

Our cheeses come from the Kaiwaka Cheese shop based in Northland and we use a variety of different ones, each with their own distinct flavour and texture. Most cheese belongs to one of four main categories, aged, soft, firm or blue. Our staple regulars include Cumin and Clove Gouda, smoked Cheddar, Old Amsterdam, Goat-young, Ricotta, Danish blue and Buffalo mozzarella.

They are delicious served with home-made (or store-bought) pear or fig paste, spicy mustard, hazelnuts, walnuts, figs and muscatels.

If you intend having a more comprehensive cheeseboard then consider adding locally sourced olives, chargrilled artichoke hearts, roasted red peppers, fresh pear or grapes and caramelised onion, to complement the cheese selection.

Keep the cheese at room temperature for at least an hour before serving, to allow them to release their various aromas.

Cocktail

SINCE 1958 **BEST MIXOLOGIST IN TOWN!!!**

COCKTAILS

... because no great story ever started with someone eating a salad.
Unknown

Similar to the growing boutique beer industry, we're in the midst of a cocktail revolution and mixologists are rediscovering the creative art of craft cocktails. The Martini, popularised by Bond films has a cult following all of its own at The Cove. After all, what other cocktail has its own glass?

Combining original flavours infused with fresh ingredients is key to making the perfect blend. We salute the classics, in particular a personal favourite, the Gin Martini.

All cocktails are made to serve one.

WILD HEART

This is a simple version of the classic whisky sour, shaken not stirred.

INGREDIENTS

50 ml (1½ oz) of whiskey
juice of 1 lemon
3 teaspoons fine raw sugar (or sugar
  syrup)

METHOD

- Pour whisky and lemon into a shaker
  and mix rigorously for 45 seconds,
  add sugar and shake again. Pour
  into a chilled rocks (short) glass.

FEISTY REDHEAD

INGREDIENTS

30 ml (1 fl oz) bourbon
15 ml (½fl oz) peach snaps
1 lime, juiced
cranberry juice
lime wedges

METHOD

- Combine ingredients in a tall glass,
  top with cranberry juice and ice.
  Garnish with a slim lime wedge.

MOJITO

INGREDIENTS

45 ml (1½ fl oz) Bacardi
handful of mint leaves
2 limes, squeezed
sprigs of mint, to serve
lime wedges, to serve

METHOD

- Combine the ingredients together
  into a tall glass and muddle for
  30 seconds. Add crushed ice and
  garnish with a mint sprig and lime
  wedge.

Note: You can muddle a cocktail
with a spoon or a pestle-like tool to
mash or grind ingredients such as
sugar or mint in the base of a glass.

COLUMBIAN MARTINI

INGREDIENTS
2 shots of Espresso
30 ml (1 fl oz) Absolut Vanilla vodka
15 ml (½ fl oz) Kahlua
10 ml (⅓ fl oz) white Crème de Cacao
dark chocolate, shaved, to garnish
espresso beans, to garnish

METHOD
- Shake all ingredients for 45 seconds and pour into a chilled martini glass. Garnish with shaved dark chocolate and espresso beans.

SAPPHIRE MARTINI

INGREDIENTS

45 ml (1½ fl oz) Bombay Sapphire (or
   alternative gin liquor)
splash Dry Vermouth
lemon twist, to serve
splash of brine (optional), to serve
juniper berries, to serve

METHOD

- Shake with ice and pour into a
  chilled martini glass.
- Serve with a lemon twist or an olive.
  Try adding a splash of the brine to
  create a dirty martini
- Add juniper berries with the lemon
  twist for added colour

THE THUNDERBIRD

INGREDIENTS

45 ml (1½ fl oz) Absolute or Grey
  Goose vodka
splash of Dry Vermouth
1 olive, to garnish

METHOD

- Vigorously mix in a shaker with ice.
- Strain into a chilled martini glass
  and add a splash of vermouth. Serve
  with an olive.

THE LONG BOARD

This cocktail packs a punch – best shared with a friend.

INGREDIENTS
10 ml (⅓ fl oz) tequila
10 ml (⅓ fl oz) vodka
10 ml (⅓ fl oz) gin
10 ml (⅓ fl oz) rum
10 ml (⅓ fl oz) Blue Curacao
10 ml (⅓ fl oz) Sprite

METHOD
- Pour liquor into a tall glass with ice and top with a mix of sprite.

INDEX

Activ8or 22
Anchovy mayonnaise 140
Angus beef sirloin and potato gratin with poached prawns 54
Apple maple crumble 162
Apple slaw 63
Apricot and berry shortcake 171
Asian dressing 52
Avocado purée 102
Baked potato gnocchi with mushroom duxelle 87
Baked saffron polenta 75
Basil Pesto 143
Beef carpaccio with truffle oil and Parmesan 51
Beetroot-cured salmon with smoked yoghurt and spiced seeds 104
Beetroot lentil salad 122
Berry coulis 153
Beurre manie 108
Beurre noisette 63
Bisque sauce 126
Black and blue tuna with miso mayonnaise and braised kelp 130
Braised beef cheeks 88
Braised kelp 130
Braised lamb 74
Butterscotch sauce 154

Cajun spice mix 141
Calf's liver with bacon and mushroom 45
Caramelised onion 72
Carli's rawnola 25
Carrot and banana cake 168
Cassoulet 70
Cauliflower, saffron and Parmesan soup 41
Cheeseboard 177
Chicken breast with couscous, feta and dukkah 69
Chilled gazpacho soup with beetroot and blue cheese 48
Chocolate fondant tart 153
Chocolate topping 161
Citrus vinaigrette 136
Columbian Martini 184
Compound butter 101
Coriander pesto 143
Cove Ceasar salad 117
Crab remoulade 114
Crab rösti with poached eggs 107
Crumbed veal with apple slaw and macadamia nuts 65
Crème brûlée 157
Cured salmon 104
Detoxicator 21
Duck cassoulet 70
Duck leg confit 70

Dukkah 76
Eggs Benedict 23
Falafel 30
Falafel and hummus platter 30
Feisty redhead 181
Fennel purée 72
Feta and sundried tomato dip 137
Garlic aioli 142
Garlic confit 140
Gluten free lemon and lime friands 165
Gnocchi 87
Goat curry 62
Granola 25
Gravlax 133
Hollandaise sauce 23
Hummus 30
Ika Mata 102
Italian-style pizza 92
Italian meringue 150
Italian sweet and sour sauce 74
Key lime pie 150
Lamb ragout with Italian sweet and sour sauce and baked saffron polenta 74
Lemon curd 159
Lemon curd mascarpone 175
Mediterranean toast 33
Miso mayonnaise 130
Mojito 182

Mushroom duxelle 87
Mushroom ragout 90
Mustard hollandaise 111
Napolitano sauce 92
Olive tapenade 142
Orange and almond cake with lemon curd mascarpone 175
Orange and fennel salad 114
Oysters with mignonette sauce 118
Pan-fried John Dory with roasted asparagus and bisque sauce 126
Panna cotta 149
Parsnip purée 126
Peachy breakfast 21
Peanut butter, chocolate and banana muffins 164
Pickled red onions 137
Pineapple crush 22
Pistachio chai muffins 173
Poached eggs 107
Poached nectarines 25
Polenta, saffron 75
Pork and rabbit rillette 58
Pork belly with roasted parsnips and salsa verde 78
Potato Alsace 81
Potato gratin 54
Ratatouille 82
Risotto 122

Roasted Highgate Hill lamb 76
Roasted parsnips 78
Romesco salsa 76
Salsa verde 78
Salted caramel slice 161
Sapphire Martini 185
Seafood chowder 108
Seared beef salad 52
Seared big eye tuna with crab remoulade 114
Seared scallops with avocado, coconut and mango salad 125
Sicilian pasta sauce 91
Smoked fish galette with potato hash 111
Smoked salmon and lentil salad 121
Smoked yoghurt 104
Smoothies 21
Snapper with citrus risotto and beetroot lentil salad 122
Spiced apple mix 162
Spiced seeds 104
Spiced sour cream 136
Spinach and ricotta gnocchi with braised beef cheek and portobello mushroom 88
Steak tartare 42
Steamed mussels 101
Stewed fruit with toasted

brioche 29
Sticky date pudding 154
Strawberry, balsamic and lemon Curd muffins 167
Sugar cured beef with coriander pesto 73
Tartare sauce 141
Tarte au citron 158
Tart pastry 158
The Thunderbird 186
Vanilla pear heaven 22
Venison with potato Alsace 81
Vita berry blast 21
Whitebait omelette 27
White chocolate panna cotta 149
Wild heart 180

ACKNOWLEDGEMENTS

Thanks to photographer Grant Rooney for his patient disposition, which made styling all the dishes for this book more enjoyable. To Lloyd, who helped make the creative process entertaining.

Additional thanks to Christine Thomson and the team at New Holland Publishers who understood the vision behind this project and helped bring it to life.

Special gratitude to my family for their constant encouragement in my various projects. Thanks to Richard, for supporting my myriad ideas and respectfully ignoring the ensuing chaos.

In appreciation of my children for their enthusiasm in our home-grown produce, bugs and all. Thanks to my daughter Carli, for her inspiration and passion for all things healthy and organic.

And finally to our friends, who make consuming delicious food and fine wine so much more enjoyable.

Lindy Davis

First published in 2016 by New Holland Publishers Pty Ltd
London • Sydney • Auckland

The Chandlery, Unit 704, 50 Westminster Bridge Road, London SE1 7QY United Kingdom 1/66
Gibbes Street, Chatswood NSW 2067 Australia
5/39 Woodside Avenue, Northcote, Auckland 0627 New Zealand

www.newhollandpublishers.com

A record of this book is held at the British Library, National Library of Australia and the New Zealand
National Library.

ISBN 9781869664541

Group Managing Director: Fiona Schultz
Publisher: Christine Thomson
Project Editor: Susie Stevens
Production Director: James Mills-Hicks
Printer: Toppan Leefung Printing Limited

Recipes supplied and created by Executive Chef, Craig Estick and Head Chef, John Salisbury at The
Cove, Waipu.
Dishes tested by Nina Backhouse and Amber Porter
Thanks to Grant and Darrell at Tipu Waterfront Accommodation, and Alan and Jenny Vaile for
providing a beautiful location to photograph seafood.

10 9 8 7 6 5 4 3 2 1

Keep up with New Holland Publishers on Facebook
www.facebook.com/NewHollandPublishers